No More Teaching
a Letter a Week

Dear Readers,

Much like the diet phenomenon *Eat This, Not That*, this series aims to replace some existing practices with approaches that are more effective—healthier, if you will—for our students. We hope to draw attention to practices that have little support in research or professional wisdom and offer alternatives that have greater support. Each text is collaboratively written by authors representing research and practice. Section 1 offers a practitioner's perspective on a practice in need of replacing and helps us understand the challenges, temptations, and misunderstandings that have led us to this ineffective approach. Section 2 provides a researcher's perspective on the lack of research to support the ineffective practice(s) and reviews research supporting better approaches. In Section 3, the author representing a practitioner's perspective gives detailed descriptions of how to implement these better practices. By the end of each book, you will understand both what not to do, and what to do, to improve student learning.

It takes courage to question one's own practice—to shift away from what you may have seen throughout your years in education and toward something new that you may have seen few if any colleagues use. We applaud you for demonstrating that courage and wish you the very best in your journey from this to that.

Best wishes,

— *Ellin Oliver Keene and Nell K. Duke, series editors*

No More Teaching a Letter a Week

Rebecca McKay

William H. Teale

HEINEMANN
Portsmouth, NH

Heinemann
361 Hanover Street
Portsmouth, NH 03801–3912
www.heinemann.com

Offices and agents throughout the world

The authors and publisher wish to thank those who have generously given permission to reprint borrowed material:

Excerpts from the Common Core State Standards © Copyright 2010. National Governors Association Center for Best Practices and Council of Chief State School Officers. All rights reserved.

Library of Congress Cataloging-in-Publication Data
McKay, Rebecca.
    No more teaching a letter a week / Rebecca McKay and William Teale.
        pages cm. – (Not this, but that)
    Includes bibliographical references.
    ISBN 978-0-325-06256-3
    1. English language—Alphabet—Study and teaching (Early childhood) I. Teale, William H. II. Title.
    LB1525.65.M45 2015
    372.46'5—dc23   2015017903

Series editors: Ellin Oliver Keene *and* Nell K. Duke
Editor: Margaret LaRaia
Development editor: Alan Huisman
Production: Hilary Goff
Interior design: Suzanne Heiser
Cover design: Lisa A. Fowler
Typesetter: Valerie Levy, Drawing Board Studios
Manufacturing: Veronica Bennett

Printed in the United States of America on acid-free paper
19   18   17   16   VP   3   4   5

CONTENTS

INTRODUCTION

ELLIN OLIVER KEENE

In many ways, this is the book that launched the Not This, But That series. Though it is not the first publication, the practice—teaching one letter at a time, one week at a time—was the first that came to mind when Nell and I began to discuss the series. We were (and are) aware of the number of preschool and kindergarten classrooms around the country in which children are introduced to the alphabet one letter at a time for a week, usually in alphabetic order, and often devoid of meaningful contexts for using the letter. This practice, like others in the series— looking up vocabulary words, taking away recess, summer-reading loss, and directionless independent reading—are ubiquitous largely because teachers haven't yet been exposed to more effective practices. Our hope for this series and, of course, for this book, is to shine a spotlight on more effective practices and to highlight the research that underlies them.

In *No More Teaching a Letter a Week*, Becky McKay, a lifelong early childhood educator, professional developer, and program director, helps us understand why it is so easy to fall into the habit of rolling out a letter a week for twenty-six straight weeks. Becky invites us to look back to our own early experiences and sure enough, there I am back in kindergarten, gluing macaroni in the shape of a letter to construction paper. There I am bending over construction paper with my Elmer's, dragging long strands of hair in the glue, macaroni dangling from the hair. I am concentrating intently, but my shaky attempts to get the lines straight for the letter *W* are spectacularly unsuccessful. I always got a good start, but the second part just never quite fit on that piece of construction paper.

Becky properly acknowledges that the task of teaching children letters and sounds is Herculean. It is extremely difficult to know where to start and how to build a coherent, developmentally appropriate approach to alphabet learning. And, in the age of Pinterest, we can become completely overwhelmed by ideas and activities that purport to teach the alphabet.

Are any of these practices aligned with the considerable body of research in this area? What were any of us learning when we struggled to get the macaroni to stay in place, and what are children learning now when they slog through one letter a week or engage in isolated activities meant to promote alphabet knowledge?

Dr. William Teale, professor and director of the Center for Literacy Development at the University of Illinois at Chicago, answers many of those questions for us in Section 2 of this book. He helps us understand the strong link between learning letters and phonemic awareness and sheds light on the "variety of factors [that] affect a child's alphabet knowledge—some related to the appearance of the letters themselves, some related to life circumstances (the name the child happens to have), some related to the child's existing knowledge from previous experience."

In the final section, Becky guides us through a wide range of practices that are aligned with research and that pave the way to a more intentional, coherent approach to teaching letters and sounds. You'll find a rich array of engaging ways to help children learn letters and sounds in meaningful contexts.

It feels gratifying to introduce this book to educators who work with young children or who are interested in understanding the foundations of language learning. Becky and Bill are steady guides toward much more promising approaches to this vital stage of children's literacy learning.

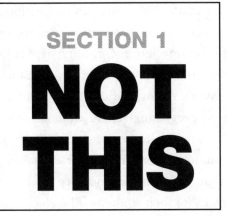

Letter-of-the-Week
Doesn't Develop Literacy

REBECCA McKAY

Teaching one letter of the alphabet a week is not the most effective practice, but if that were all that I needed to tell you, we wouldn't need this book. It is *not* an effective approach but it manages to attract new generations of teachers each year (an online search reveals 144 million sites that offer resources to teach letter of the week). If we're going to give up the practice—and I'm hoping that by the end of this book, you'll feel well prepared to do that—first we need to acknowledge why we have such a hard time letting it go.

A Tidy Practice for Grown-Ups

Teaching a letter a week is appealing to many teachers. Why?

First, the responsibility of ensuring that all of their students learn to read and write can, at times, feel overwhelming. When we let that worry sink into our bones, it can sometimes dictate our behavior, making us less thoughtful than we would normally be. And, so, the alphabet sequence presents itself as if it were a list of skills. This week, we will "do A" and we'll include three activities that include the letter . . . in some way. The process feels manageable, and we tell ourselves that by the time we reach the letter Z, twenty-six weeks into the school year, our students will be well on their way to reading. We've done A to Z. When we say we've covered the "A to Z" of anything, it means that we've covered everything. There are book titles that promise to inform you of the A to Z of corporate responsibility, the A to Z of fantasy literature. But does A to Z truly cover everything?

It's also true that many early elementary teachers value tactile and creative experiences for their students. The glue, macaroni, beans, and song making, vestiges of traditional letter-of-the-week instruction, can feel like a hands-on way to teach the alphabet. But during these activities, children may or may not be thinking deeply about the letter they are supposed to be learning.

All those hands-on activities may create "evidence" of children's learning that we can send home to parents. The feather F on the family refrigerator is taken down to make room for the glitter glue G. Teaching a letter a week may seem like a way to invite family to participate by discussing the featured letter over dinner or to prepare letter bags containing objects whose names start with that week's letter. A number of activities like these may feel like instruction, and the collaborative nature of the singing, talking, and gathering can be wonderful. But, does teaching one letter a week help our children become readers and writers?

What Does "Doing *C*" Mean, Anyway?

We teachers sometimes work unnecessarily hard when what's needed is not this degree of elbow grease but more information. Working smarter, not harder. Teaching letter-of-the-week typically involves a lot of activity and can even be expensive; I spent quite a bit of time and money to prepare for my letter-of-the-week instruction. And, I even had research citations to support my practice: students who demonstrate phonemic awareness and alphabet recognition are more likely to become successful readers (Adams 1990; Share et al. 1987; National Reading Panel 2000). But let's note what was missing. The research *didn't* say:

- that children learn the names and sounds of letters by letter-themed activities, such as
    - gluing cotton balls on large construction paper *C*s
    - eating foods or bringing in objects from home that start with *C*, or
- that teaching one letter each week in ABC order is an effective sequence and pacing for alphabet learning
- that teaching one letter each week is a better practice than other ways of teaching alphabet knowledge.

Let's take a moment to consider the gap between intent and practice. My intent was to invite children into the world of print through alphabet learning, but there were some important questions I should have been asking:

- Although I did expose children to the letter *C*, was I *explicitly* teaching its name, functions, and sound associations?
- Were children gaining more than the awareness that *C* is a thing without understanding the purpose of letters, both specifically and generally?

Instead of documentable learning, here's what remained of my practice: some wisps of cotton in my hair and images of letters on construction paper (that may have briefly guest starred on the family refrigerator). Some children likely inferred the relationship between letter symbols and their function, but there wasn't much evidence of it in my teaching. And, this absence meant that many children left my classroom lacking not only essential knowledge to succeed but also a meaningful invitation to the world of literacy.

How do children acquire alphabet knowledge?

see Section 2, pages 11–18

"I Wish I Had Known"

In retrospect, I wish I had known how children acquire alphabet knowledge, so that I could plan around that, rather than around which letter-of-the-week activities I would choose for *C*. In over thirty years of teaching and coaching teachers, "I wish I had known" is one of the responses I hear most from teachers because they so fervently want to do right by students. I know the grief and guilt one feels at recognizing one's own ineffective practice. It's the realization that—opposite of our intention—we've taken important time and learning away from children. Teaching is always an approximation; there's always new learning that becomes an I-wish-I-had-known.

Two teachers in a midsized Georgia school district, Quleria Persons and Berderia Fuller, sensed there was much more to know about alphabet knowledge and decided to lead colleagues in a study group. They read the latest professional books and research articles, talked with colleagues, and studied the children in their classrooms. There was a lot that these teachers didn't know when they began their work. What they did have was a belief that, by reading professional resources and through talking to other teachers, they could teach alphabet knowledge to every child in their classroom and they'd find the evidence to prove it, day to day and across the year. They began their inquiry into better teaching of alphabet knowledge with the following questions:

What can that look like in practice?

see Section 3 for the details

- What are the skills that define alphabet knowledge?
- How can teachers situate alphabet learning in a meaningful context and structure time so that students receive explicit instruction and varied experiences for practice?

How can teachers assess teaching for effectiveness and identify what to do if children aren't acquiring alphabet knowledge? Over a cup of coffee, I spoke with Joe, a remarkable kindergarten teacher and early childhood expert who participated in Quleria's and Berderia's study group. We shared our respective I-wish-I-had-knowns related to alphabet learning. Joe told me how much he wished he had known about the importance of segmenting and blending sounds in words. "Although I modeled it in writing workshop, I didn't spend enough time explicitly teaching how to do it, and I didn't even know about the different routines for blending." By believing that he, like all of us, might benefit from learning more, Joe didn't place limits on his practice, and he became outstanding. He gained the knowledge about teaching letters and sounds that he needed.

We have to remember that we're not in this work alone and that when we rely solely on the pedagogy from our teaching certification program, we're putting limits on ourselves, on our teaching, and on the learning our students can do. If we embrace the identity of voracious students of pedagogy, like Quleria, Berderia, and Joe, we clear our instruction of the thorny snare of ineffective practice. Research can be our helpmate, our tool; it provides a framework that we can build our practice around and a way of measuring whether our practice is effective. In Section 2, Bill shares his synthesis of the latest research that explains why alphabet knowledge is necessary and how children acquire alphabet knowledge. He highlights what research tells us about effective and ineffective practice. I return in Section 3 to share examples of better practices for alphabet learning that I hope will inspire your own. We can do better than letter-of-the-week. I think you'll find the alternative practices much more fun, meaningful, and effective, so let's not waste any more time. On to the research!

WHY NOT? WHAT WORKS?

What Research Says About the Sense and Sounds of Letters

WILLIAM H. TEALE

When it comes to reading in English, more research by far has been conducted on beginning reading than on any other phase of development. The research is deep and wide, and one thing is clear: research evidence does not support a letter-of-the-week approach to instruction about letters and letter sounds. But, as Becky explained through examples like the volume of Internet hits for "letter-of-the-week" instruction, the information isn't getting to teachers. We're hoping that an examination of the evidence related to the following three key issues can be used by everyone to convince all early childhood and primary-grade teachers and educational leaders to eschew, abandon, and otherwise shun letter of the week in favor of instruction that helps all children learn what they need to know about letters and letter sounds in ways that promote early reading and writing achievement:

- why alphabet knowledge is necessary

- how we acquire alphabet knowledge
- how we should teach the alphabet in early childhood classrooms.

Alphabet Knowledge and Why It's Necessary

Although there are other important areas critical to understanding how children learn to read, such as cognitive abilities, phonological awareness, and oral language development (National Early Literacy Panel 2008), we can't write or read words without understanding what a letter is. Knowing not just letter names but the sounds and meaning that letters carry is essential to children's early literacy. It is significant in emerging literacy (Teale et al. 2009; Whitehurst and Lonigan 1998) and early conventional reading (Adams 2010; Ehri and Roberts 2006) and a very strong predictor of later reading ability (Hammill 2004; National Early Literacy Panel 2008; Scarborough 1998; Schatschneider et al. 2004) or reading difficulty (Catts et al. 2002; Burgess and Lonigan 1998; McBride-Chang 1999; National Early Literacy Panel 2008; Piasta and Wagner 2010; Wagner, Torgesen, and Rashotte 1994). Knowing the alphabet makes a unique contribution in the process of learning to read; even though it's a means to being able to read and write, it's important in its own right.

Learning Letter Names and Sounds: What's Involved?

In the United States it is common practice to teach young children the names of the letters of the English alphabet. At its most basic, this is the ability to say /ei/ in response to *A* or *a*, /bee/ in response to *B* or *b*, and so forth. Other aspects of knowing letter names include the ability to write particular letters when the letter's name is uttered, pick out a particular letter from an array of letters when that letter name is uttered, or form the letter. A child's knowledge of letter names is typically assessed by presenting each letter separately and asking the child to name the letter or by pointing to an individual letter in an array and asking the child to name it.

The sound a written letter represents is its most typically associated phoneme (or in some cases phonemes). This is tricky in English, because, for one thing, a particular letter may be associated with different sounds depending on the word in which it appears (especially vowels, e.g., long versus short vowels, but also some consonants, depending on their position in a word and surrounding letters, e.g., *g* in *gourd* versus *giant*). Also, when going from sound to letter, a particular sound (phoneme) may be represented in writing by different letters (the /s/ sound might be an *s* or a *c*). (This doesn't even consider that sometimes a particular two-letter combination results in one sound: *ch* = /č/, for example.) However, young children's knowledge of letter sounds is typically conceptualized and assessed by the sound (or sounds in the case of vowels and some consonants) most often associated with that letter when it is read.

Therefore, in English, the letter name–typical sound relationship is a primary consideration. The typical sound a letter represents is just that, *a* sound, or in linguistic terms, a *phoneme* (the smallest distinctive sounds in a language). But here's the thing: Although some letter names constitute a single phoneme, most contain two phonemes, and some contain more than two. The vowel letter names *a, e, i,* and *o* each constitute one sound. The letter names for most consonants and the vowel *u* contain two sounds. For example, *b, k,* and *f* are /bi/, /kay/, and / f/, respectively. The letters *h, q, w,* and *x* all have names that contain more than two sounds. So the child has to be able to separate the sounds in the letter name (a process that requires phonological awareness skill) and figure out which of the two or three sounds is the one commonly associated with the letter.

Making things even more complicated are the sound position relationships between the phonemes that constitute the letter name and those that constitute the most typical sound associated with the letter. In some multiphoneme letter names, the typical sound comes first (*b, c, d, g, j, k, p, q, t, v, z*); in others it comes second (*f, l, m, n, s, x*); and then there are those (*h, w, y*) that do not even contain the typical sound.

Considering these complicated letter–sound relationships, we begin to see what young children face when sorting out the beginnings of decoding in their early literacy learning. These characteristics of letter name–letter sound relationships are therefore built into the design of many research studies related to learning the alphabet.

Most research that examines young children's knowledge of the alphabet provides information about the relationship between the children's knowledge of letter names and letter sounds, even if it is not the central focus of the study (Roberts 2013). Although inconsistent letter name–letter sound relationships can confuse children, it has long been recognized that knowing letter names is nevertheless positively associated with knowing letter sounds (Lomax and McGee 1987; Richgels 1986; Worden and Boettcher 1990). In addition, more recently experimental evidence has accumulated to indicate that letter name knowledge makes a unique contribution to children's understanding of English alphabetic principles and later reading skill. Piasta, Purpura, and Wagner (2010), for example, randomly assigned preschool children to one of three instructional groups: letter name and letter sound, letter sound only, or treated control (instruction on numbers). They found that, after thirty-four fifteen-minute lessons, children taught in the letter name–letter sound condition showed the greatest advantage in alphabet learning. So, although the real goal is for children to understand letter–sound relationships, learning letter names contributes to that process.

> **How can we ground alphabet knowledge in authentic literacy?**
>
> see Section 3, page 33

Learning Letter Names and Sounds: Interrelationships

In practical terms, these two aspects of alphabet knowledge—letter names and letter sounds—are closely related. Children who know lots of letter names also tend to score better in their knowledge of letter sounds; children who know only a few letter names typically do not know many letter sounds. (You've almost certainly experienced this in your classroom.)

Research into this question has been interpreted in different ways:

- Knowing letter names helps children learn letter sounds because most letter names contain the phoneme associated with that letter (Walsh, Price, and Gillingham 1988; Ehri 1983; Treiman et al. 1998).
- Knowing letter names is associated with other cognitive abilities (language ability, IQ) involved in early reading (Evans et al. 2006).
- Knowing letter names facilitates phonological awareness (Share 2004).

A key question for the teacher is "If I spend time helping children learn letter names and sounds, will it pay off in other areas of early literacy development?" Based on the existing research, the answer is yes. The relationship between knowing the alphabet and later reading achievement is most likely causal (Lonigan, Burgess, and Anthony 2000; Share 2004). More precisely, children's ability to learn letter–sound correspondence appears directly linked to knowing the letter names (McBride-Chang 1999; Share 2004; Treiman et al. 1998). Young children use their knowledge of letter names to learn letter sounds (Piasta and Wagner 2010; Treiman et al. 1998) and knowing letter names and sounds is foundational to other aspects of early literacy development.

In terms of young children's literacy activities, one need only examine children's invented spelling (Read 1971; Schickedanz and Casbergue 2009) to see that letter name knowledge helps with other aspects of early literacy learning. There are patterns to their "misspellings": many preschoolers and kindergartners use the letter name to represent the phoneme they hear in a word—*BIK* for *bike*; *FEL* for *feel*; *FRAD* for *friend*; and even *HRK* for *truck*. This strategy draws upon the letter name–letter sound link present in many of the alphabet letter names, enabling young children to productively participate in early writing activities, which has been shown to positively contribute to reading achievement (Richgels 1995, 2001; Clarke 1988).

How Young Children Learn the Alphabet

In North America, learning the alphabet is an important aspect of young children's development. For many years, it was central to the kindergarten curriculum; now it is also widely considered a task for preschoolers (Teale 1995; McGee and Richgels 2012). The Head Start Child Outcomes Framework Standards (U.S. Department of Health and Human Services 2014) require that each child be able to identify "at least ten letters of the alphabet, especially those in his/her own name." The major preschool literacy program funded by the U.S. Department of Education during the first decade of the twenty-first century, Early Reading First, had explicit goals for learning letter names and sounds (U.S. Department of Education 2014). Learning the alphabet remains a goal for virtually all kindergartens in the United States and features prominently in the English Language Arts standards of the Common Core State Standards for kindergarten (Common Core State Standards Initiative 2015): Reading Standards—Foundational Skills (Kindergarten): Print Concepts, 1d: "Recognize and name all upper- and lowercase letters of the alphabet." Most kindergarten curricula are designed with the goal of having children "learn their letters and sounds" during the first part of the school year.

Research studies consistently demonstrate that children typically learn the letter name before they learn its associated sound (Blaiklock 2004; de Abreu and Cardoso-Martins 1998; Huang and Invernizzi 2012; Mason 1980; Treiman et al. 1998)—unless they initially experience classroom teaching about the alphabet in programs that deliberately avoid teaching letter names and teach common letter sounds instead (e.g., most Montessori classrooms). Research undertaken at the University of Illinois at Chicago related to implementing Early Reading First in Chicago-area prekindergarten classrooms (University of Illinois at Chicago 2008) also reveals that children typically learn a letter name before they learn the sound associated with that letter. (Figure 2–1 shows beginning-of-the-year PALS letter name and letter sound scores for one class of fourteen preschoolers.)

Figure 2–1 Pre-K Children's Entering Alphabet Knowledge

Name	Uppercase Letters	Lowercase Letters	Letter Sounds
Evelyn	4	4	1
Juan	23	15	3
Xochil	26	23	1
Bernard	0	0	0
Luigi	5	1	2
Miguel	22	21	10
Reginald	11	1	2
Tameka	26	16	12
Juan	23	13	2
Alyssa	10	2	0
Peter	26	21	2
Jackson	5	2	0
Thomas	2	0	0
Veronica	26	26	18

Research provides no clear reason as to why letter name knowledge typically precedes letter–sound knowledge. It could be that developing letter–sound knowledge is more challenging, or it could be a result of the cultural importance placed on learning the names of alphabet letters (having children spell their names, sing the alphabet song, and so forth);

more likely it is a combination of both. For practical classroom purposes, why may not matter as much as knowing the pattern exists.

Knowing the Alphabet Is Linked to Phonological Awareness

Phonological awareness is fundamentally an oral language skill. It refers to the ability to isolate the various, increasingly smaller components of oral speech: syllables, onsets, and rimes (*onset*, the initial consonantal segment of a word [before the vowel]; and *rime*, the vowel and following consonant[s]: *t-op*; *b-eat*; *ch-amp*; and so on), and, finally, phonemes. Phonological awareness is an essential element in learning to read an alphabetic orthography like English, Spanish, or Turkish. A substantial body of research (e.g., Foy and Mann 2006; National Reading Panel 2000; Stahl and Murray 1994; Vellutino and Scanlon 1987; Wagner, Torgesen, and Rashotte 1994) has established a close connection—both statistically and in terms of practical importance—between children's phonological awareness and their knowledge of the alphabet. Interconnections between phonological awareness and letter knowledge foster early literacy. For example, in their early writing attempts children link their developing ability to hear smaller and smaller components of oral speech to their knowledge of letter names as they progress through speech-print connection phases, from prephonemic (*DRN* for bike) to early phonemic (*B* or *BK* for *bike*) to connecting letter names with letter sounds (*BIK* for *bike*) (Ehri and Roberts 2006; Schickedanz and Casbergue 2009). In addition, it has been found that phonological awareness is associated with word recognition ability as children move from emergent reading into conventional reading in kindergarten or first grade (Ehri and McCormick 2013). Thus, time spent developing children's phonological awareness in pre-K and K has long-term as well as immediate benefits.

As it commonly occurs in early childhood classrooms, alphabet instruction requires phonological awareness. That is to say, books, media, apps, and teachers often teach key words for particular letters—

"*a* is for *apple*"—but for such a concept to be meaningful to children, they have to have the phonological awareness skills to break *apple* into its constituent sounds, in this case to segment (isolate and hear) the short *a* sound at the beginning of the word. In many cases, children may have even memorized these letter–key word associations and can chant them along with other classmates during lessons: "*B* is for *bear*, /buh/, /buh/, /buh/; *C* is for *car*, /kuh/, /kuh/, /kuh/. . . . " But, often individual children can't actually use such key words to identify letter sounds because they don't hear the individual sound in the key word that they are supposed to associate with the letter—they are merely repeating what they have heard over and over.

Alphabet Knowledge: What Children Learn, and When and Why They Learn It

This is a big—and complicated—topic. To deliver effective and efficient alphabet instruction, all early childhood teachers need to understand which letter names and letter sounds are easier and which are more complicated. What about uppercase letters versus lowercase letters? What is the relationship between the different "types" of letter names (the typical letter–sound phoneme occurs initially, in the final position, or not at all) and learning letter sounds? Research has addressed these questions.

Let's begin with the "difficulty" of different letter–sound relationships and the order in which young children typically learn the alphabet. UIC's Early Reading First programs (University of Illinois at Chicago 2008) collected data over a seven-year period on 710 prekindergarten children and their knowledge of uppercase letters, lowercase letters, and the most commonly associated letter sounds. Figure 2–2 shows what these children knew about each letter of the alphabet as they entered pre-K. (In Early Reading First classrooms at least 75 percent of the children qualified for a free or reduced-price lunch.)

Figure 2–2 Entering Kindergartners' Letter and Letter–Sound Knowledge

Uppercase	Percent of Children Knowing	Lowercase	Percent of Children Knowing	Letter Sound	Percent of Children Knowing
O	63.9	o	52.7	S	32.4
B	54.9	x	43.2	B	28.0
X	50.3	s	39.4	U	22.7
A	49.6	w	37.5	L	18.2
S	43.5	c	36.8	P	18.2
M	42.5	i	35.4	G	17.7
W	42.3	k	33.7	Z	16.8
R	42.0	z	32.1	E	16.2
C	41.7	m	30.8	K	14.6
L	41.7	e	30.3	A	14.5
E	40.3	p	30.1	W	13.0
T	37.9	j	28.9	Q	12.4
D	37.2	y	28.6	D	12.3
H	37.2	r	28.5	O	10.7
P	37.0	v	24.6	M	9.7
K	36.8	u	23.8	N	9.0
Q	36.1	t	23.5	F	8.6
Z	35.6	a	23.4	X	8.2
J	35.4	f	23.0	H	6.6
G	34.8	b	22.4	J	4.2
I	34.2	h	19.0	V	3.8

(continues)

Figure 2–2 (*continued*)

Uppercase	Percent of Children Knowing	Lowercase	Percent of Children Knowing	Letter Sound	Percent of Children Knowing
Y	34.2	n	17.0	Y	3.2
F	33.8	g	16.8	R	1.5
U	33.4	l	15.1	C	1.4
N	30.7	d	13.4	I	1.3
V	25.2	q	12.0	T	0.6

The table reveals several interesting things. First, a sizeable portion of children whose family income level suggests that they should be at risk for low reading achievement begin their school experience already having a degree of alphabet knowledge. For instance, every uppercase letter is known by a quarter or more of the children. In addition, across the entire group, at least some children demonstrated knowledge of each lowercase letter, but fewer than for uppercase letters (a finding echoed in all research regarding alphabet knowledge I'm aware of and explicitly noted in Smythe et al. [1971] and Worden and Boettcher [1990]). The children also have some knowledge of letter–sound relationships on which needed instruction can be based. It can also be seen that some letters are "easier" than others. Uppercase *O, B, X,* and *A* are recognized by almost half of the children. The pattern changes with lowercase letters: the *b* is much more of a challenge (no doubt because it shares so many distinctive features with the "confusable" *d, p,* and *q*). The most widely known letter–sound relationships are both similar to and different from letter name knowledge. Other patterns evident in these children could also be pointed out, and other large-scale studies of letter and letter–sound knowledge (e.g., Bowles et al. 2014; Piasta and Wagner 2010) can be used to give a sense of typically easier and harder uppercase, lowercase, and letter–sound knowledge; but a key point is that there *are* patterns to how young children learn the alphabet and those patterns are directly relevant to instruction, a point that is explicitly addressed in Section 3 with respect to the order and timing of teaching about letters and letter sounds.

For an additional perspective on the what, when, and why of young children's alphabet learning, consider research by Justice et al. (2006) of 339 four-year-olds assessed during the early part of prekindergarten. This study is one of the few direct investigations of the order in which children learn the alphabet. The researchers examined four hypotheses related to learning letter names, the following three of which are most directly relevant to our discussion here: (1) own name advantage—children learn first the letters that appear in their own names; (2) letter order—letters occurring earlier in the alphabet are learned before those occurring later; and (3) letter name pronunciation—children learn first the letter names heard in the names' pronunciation. They found that the letters *B, X, O,* and *A* were known by the largest number of children (roughly half) and *V, U, N,* and *G* were known by the fewest (13–17 percent). Their findings regarding the three investigated hypotheses were:

- *Own name.* Letters in a child's first name or nickname were known at a higher rate than letters not in a child's first name or nickname; the first letter of a child's first name or nickname was learned especially quickly.
- *Letter order.* This had a small but reliable effect; letters in the first half of the alphabet were recognized at a slightly higher rate than letters in the second half of the alphabet.
- *Letter name pronunciation.* There was no significantly better facility learning letter names that started or ended with the phoneme in the initial or final position of the letter's pronunciation, but letter names for those that contained the phoneme were recognized more frequently than those that did not.

> **The research tells us that there is not one perfect sequence of instruction for alphabet knowledge, so how can we decide what to teach when?**
>
> see Section 3, page 34

Let us consider one more study that examined patterns in young children's developing alphabet knowledge. Turnbull et al. (2010) focused specifically on preschoolers' lowercase alphabet knowledge, attempting to understand the influence of four factors: uppercase familiarity, uppercase–lowercase similarity, own name advantage, and how often a letter appears in print. They found uppercase familiarity to be the strongest predictor: if a child knew the uppercase of a particular letter, the child was sixteen times more likely to know the lowercase of that same letter. This was especially true if the lowercase appearance of the letter was similar to that of the uppercase. And it also helped lowercase recognition if the letter was in the child's name and the child knew it in the uppercase. I cite this study because it helps demonstrate that a variety of factors affect a child's alphabet knowledge—some related to the appearance of the letters themselves, some related to life circumstances (the name the child happens to have), some related to the child's existing knowledge from previous experience, and so forth.

It doesn't take long for any teacher of young children to recognize that some letters are more difficult for most children to learn, that different children come to instruction with different degrees and types of alphabet knowledge, that different children learn in different time frames, and that some aspects of alphabet knowledge are more difficult for children than others. Research is providing specifics that help teachers know typical (and atypical) patterns for what is happening when.

Data such as those in Figure 2–2 and from the research studies just discussed (along with many, many other studies that could be cited) indicate that, when it comes to classroom practice, (1) not every letter requires the same instructional attention; (2) whole-class instruction focused on a particular letter is inefficient because some children in any kindergarten classroom will have already learned many letters; and (3) no one sequence for teaching letters and their associated sounds is optimal for all our children.

How Many Letters and Letter Sounds Should Young Children Know, and by When?

This question becomes important in light of the differing standards for alphabet knowledge that can be found for preschoolers:

- Alaska, Alabama, Arizona, South Dakota—at least 10 letters
- Indiana—13 uppercase letters
- The Head Start Outcomes Framework—"Identifies at least 10 letters of the alphabet, especially those in their own name"
- Early Reading First Performance Targets—16 to 19 letters.

You get the picture—standards for alphabet knowledge vary considerably. What does research say about what standards should be? There is as yet no comprehensive answer to this question, in part because the question itself is multifaceted: Is it how many to be considered not at risk? To be successful in reading at third grade? At first grade? And so forth. . . . It is also the case that few studies have addressed this question directly. The best indicator we have to date comes from research conducted by Piasta, Petscher, and Justice (2012). They investigated the diagnostic efficiency of various upper- and lowercase letter-naming standards for 371 preschoolers, and one particular question in the study attempted to identify "optimal benchmarks." Findings indicated that an end-of-preschool/beginning of kindergarten benchmark of ten letters was adequate to determine negative predictive power (the vast majority of children reaching this benchmark would not be at risk for low literacy achievement in grade 1), but also that optimal benchmarks were eighteen uppercase letters and fifteen lowercase letters when considering the three later grade literacy outcomes of letter–word identification, spelling, and passage comprehension. Thus, Piasta, Petscher, and Justice (2012) advocate setting higher end-of-preschool benchmarks than those typically appearing in state early learning standards or Head Start standards.

Overall conclusions based on research about how young children learn the alphabet are outlined in Figure 2–3.

Figure 2–3 Research Conclusions About How Young Children Learn the Alphabet

Summary Research Conclusions About How Young Children Learn the Alphabet	Therefore: Why a Letter-of-the-Week Approach Is Not Warranted
Various letter features, as well as students' attributes like their name, affect which letters children learn earlier or later and find easier or more difficult.	Letter-of-the-week approaches each of the twenty-six letters equally in terms of the learning activities provided for children and the amount of time allocated to instruction. Some letter-of-the-week programs present the letters in alphabetical order.
The pattern for learning the alphabet varies from child to child, but how young children learn letter names and letter sounds is neither random nor completely idiosyncratic. There are patterns to this learning that we can use to plan our instruction.	A letter-of-the-week approach treats every child in the classroom the same with respect to the *what* and *when* of alphabet knowledge. Such an approach completely ignores a child's prior knowledge and what assessment data indicate as best next steps for individual children and groups of children in the class. This makes instruction inefficient at best and ineffective at worst.
There are statistically and practically significant connections between phonological awareness and learning the alphabet.	A letter-of-the-week approach is problematic if it focuses mainly on letter naming and letter–sound activities without also including sufficient systematic instructional attention to phonological awareness in conjunction with letter knowledge.

How We Should Teach the Alphabet in Early Childhood Classrooms

Clearly, learning the alphabet is extremely important, and research findings related to typical and atypical developmental patterns in learning the alphabet, as well as the patterns and means by which children learn letter names and letter sounds, can help us determine appropriate early literacy instruction. These findings strongly suggest that a letter-of-the-week approach is not an effective way to reach all the children in the classroom.

Educators have *many* ideas about what, how, and when we should teach young children the alphabet and letter–sound correspondence. My Google search of "how to teach the English alphabet to children aged four to six" brought 54.7 million results (I opted not to look at all of them!): there are books, YouTube videos, blogs, sections, articles, full curriculums, and more out there in abundance. Publishers extol their programs; teachers offer lessons they use in their classrooms; parents share their ideas; researchers document studies of interventions conducted in "regular" preschool or kindergarten classrooms or with groups of children experiencing moderate or severe difficulties learning to read. I have no doubt that *every one of them worked*—for some child, at some time, in some instance. But research studies about the specific elements of effective alphabet instruction probably number fewer than a hundred.

The long and short of it is this: there is less definitive information about effective strategies for teaching the alphabet than there is about how children learn the alphabet. The reasons for this state of affairs have much to do with how research has been and is being funded and conducted in the worlds of academia, public and private education, and government; but let us stay focused on the practical implications for classroom practice. With that end in mind, we find that available research does allow us to draw a few important conclusions about teaching and learning the alphabet. First, however, I need to mention two caveats:

- there is an overrepresentation in this body of research on children who are "struggling" or "at risk for low reading achievement"
- virtually all the studies focus on explicit instruction.

These factors have a bearing on the role of alphabet instruction and how it should be presented. In one sense, learning the alphabet is not easy: the English alphabet comprises forty different shapes (Roberts 2009) whose names are arbitrary. On the other hand, some children learn the alphabet as a result of everyday interactions in their homes and communities. There has been considerable debate over the years (Bredekamp 1987; Copple and Bredekamp 2010) about the appropriateness of and nature of early literacy instruction—what constitutes appropriate instruction related to a skill like knowing the alphabet and what is "developmentally inappropriate"?

Keeping these factors in mind and considering the accumulated evidence related to alphabet knowledge instruction represented in the Roberts and Vadasy (2013) and Piasta and Wagner (2010) reviews, studies by Jones and Reutzel (2012) and Jones, Clark, and Reutzel (2012) not included in those reviews, and research reviewed by the What Works Clearinghouse (WWC; a U.S. Department of Education/ Institute of Education Sciences Web-based repository that reviews "high-quality research" on "programs, products, practices, and policies in education" to "provide educators with the information they need to make evidence-based decisions"; http://ies.ed.gov/ncee/wwc/), we can use the following points to guide our classroom assessment and instructional practices.

Intentional and Systematic Instruction

Although some children learn quite a bit about the alphabet informally in their homes, communities, and child-care settings, most children need (and all children benefit from) intentional, systematic school instruction in the process of becoming fluent in naming letters and understanding letter–sound relationships. This is especially true for children at risk for reading underachievement (National Assessment of Educational Progress 2013). Children who do not have literacy-rich homes or communities depend on their school experiences to develop the literacy skills necessary for school success; research clearly indicates that an approach that intentionally and systematically teaches them letter names and letter sounds has significantly better results than one that approaches learning the alphabet indirectly (National Reading Panel 2000; National Early Literacy Panel 2008).

However, it is equally important to point out that *intentionally* and *systematically* does not necessarily mean scripted instruction (one type of which is commonly called *Direct Instruction*) in which the cognitive skill of alphabet knowledge is broken down into small units, sequenced deliberately, and each of the units is taught explicitly in that sequence to all the children in the classroom. In its review of research related to direct instruction in literacy, the WWC concluded that Direct Instruction "was found to have no discernible effects on [children's] oral language [or] print knowledge" (Institute of Education Sciences 2007). As research syntheses such as those from the National Reading Panel and the National Early Literacy Panel clearly indicate, having a plan and systematically instructing children about the alphabet is a good idea (and better in terms of child learning outcomes than an "incidental" or "as-needed" approach), but a whole-class, scripted approach to such instruction has not been proven to be an effective form of instruction.

No One Instructional Approach Is Best, but There Are Recommended Practices

Although teaching the alphabet intentionally and systematically has been broadly established as significantly more effective than informal, catch-as-catch-can approaches, findings also show that no particular program—either formally published or available informally on the Internet—has proven most effective (National Reading Panel 2000; National Early Literacy Panel 2008; Phillips and Piasta 2013). Nevertheless, a number of features recur in effective instruction:

- *Exposure and practice: repeated, varied, and not too much.* Piasta and Wagner (2010) analyzed sixty-three studies on teaching and learning the alphabet. One finding was that more instruction is generally better. Likewise, the work of Jones and Reutzel (2012), Justice, et al. (2006), and McBride-Chang (1999) indicates that frequent exposure and repetitive practice are significant factors in learning the alphabet. In these approaches, letters are not taught once or twice, but many times. Jones and Reutzel provided instruction on a different letter each day, cycling through the alphabet five times or more, with a different emphasis each time and with 10–20 percent of classroom instruction devoted to review. The other important facet of their work was careful assessment: once a child had mastered a letter, he or she was given no further instruction on that letter. These studies reveal three significant features: (1) lots of exposure to and practice with letters; (2) varied practice (not doing the same thing over and over); and (3) no more instruction than needed. A teacher should be sure a child has as many experiences and as much practice as needed, but once she or he knows a letter name and its associated sound(s), there is no sense delivering more instruction on that letter and sound. It's time to move on to letters the child doesn't know and to devote instruction to the other important aspects of early literacy. The "Goldilocks principle" is appropriate here: not too little; not too much.

- *Small-group instruction.* The National Early Literacy Panel (2008) and Piasta and Wagner (2010) found that small-group instruction was more effective than either individualized instruction or whole-class instruction in developing young children's knowledge of the alphabet. This doesn't mean that individual or whole-class instruction should never be used when teaching letter names or letter sounds. But small-group instruction is the most effective and time-efficient, given the fact that, as detailed above, children in any classroom have differential knowledge about letters and letter sounds.

- *Multicomponent instruction.* In 2006, WWC indicated that letter knowledge had positive effects on young children's print knowledge and potentially positive effects on their phonological processing and early reading/writing *when paired with phonological awareness training* (Institute of Education Sciences 2006). Numerous studies have coupled teaching the alphabet and teaching phonological awareness. Fifty-three of the sixty-three studies reviewed by Piasta and Wagner (2010) combined teaching the alphabet with other instructional components, most often phonological awareness.

Phonological awareness is easily a whole book by itself, and the research on it is plentiful (see Bus and van IJzendoorn 1999; Ehri et al. [2001] and Melby-Lervåg, Lyster, and Hulme [2012] for overviews). Like alphabet knowledge, phonological awareness is one of the strongest early childhood predictors of later reading achievement (National Reading Panel 2000; National Early Literacy Panel 2008). A recurrent finding in studies that examine teaching the alphabet along with teaching phonological awareness is that concurrent attention to both has significantly more impact on early development of the concept of language as a code than either component taught separately. Therefore, instruction related to the code aspects of early literacy should have several components: teaching letter names should be related to teaching letter sounds should be related to teaching phonological awareness should be related to teaching print awareness. The other component that research suggests can profitably be made part of alphabet instruction is letter formation. Children recognize letters by attending to, and ultimately quickly recognizing, their "distinctive features" (Gibson and Levin 1975), features that also need to be attended to when forming/writing the letters: straight lines, diagonal lines, curved lines, intersections, and so forth. Some letters have very individual distinctive features—*X/x*, for example. Other letters share many distinctive features and are therefore typically more difficult to recognize or form (*p*, *b*, *d*, *q* or *G* and *C*). The motor sequence experienced forming these letters (muscle memory) can help in learning the alphabet, because it emphasizes the critical differences among the letters (Hayes 1982). Producing the letters helps children recognize them.

For an activity that helps children practice in a fun, playful way

see Section 3, page 68

- *Considering the order of teaching letters.* Commercial and teacher-developed programs for teaching the letters of the alphabet choose various sequences for doing so. Many continue to use the traditional approach of teaching the letters in alphabetical order, starting with *A* and proceeding through *Z*. Others teach the "easy" consonants first. A number of programs begin with a mixture of consonants and short vowels, so children are able to put letters together to form words early on. There is no evidence showing the superiority of one order over another. However, the research discussed under "Alphabet Knowledge: What Children Learn and When and Why They Learn It" on pages 14–18 found that letters in children's names are particularly salient; some letters are "easier" because they have regular letter–sound relationships, the visual features of some letters make them more memorable, and so forth. Research findings like these were no doubt considered in determining the teaching cycles in the Jones and Reutzel (2012) instructional program. Therefore, although no one particular order is clearly superior, we can take advantage of these aspects of children's learning in planning instruction that also provides varied and repeated experiences.

Jones, Clark, and Reutzel (2102), for example, had significant success in thirteen kindergarten classrooms teaching all twenty-six letters over a five-week period. Their approach to order of instruction was multifaceted. Each of their six instructional cycles presented letters in different orders, depending on the particular advantage of alphabet learning centered on during that cycle (own name advantage, alphabetical order advantage, letter name–letter sound relationship advantage, letter frequency advantage, consonant phoneme acquisition order advantage, or distinctive visual features advantage). For example, the letter name–letter sound relationship advantage cycle began with the consonant letters that have the letter sound at the beginning of the letter name (b, d, j, k, p, t, v, z), followed by consonant letters with the sound at the end of the letter name (f, l, m, n, r, x). Consonants with no letter name–letter sound association (h, q, w, y) or with more than one sound (c, g, s) were taught repeatedly throughout the week focused on letter name–letter sound advantage and received more instructional time because they are typically more challenging to learn. During the letter frequency cycle, letters were taught from most to least frequent: consonants ($r, t, n, s, l, c, d, p, m, b, f, v, g, h, k, w, x, z, j, q, y$) and vowels ($i, a, e, o, u$). Thus, children experienced instruction in multiple orders, thereby enhancing their flexibility in thinking about letters and the associated sounds.

- *Pace—teaching letters early and intensely and to the degree needed by each individual child.* It's time to debunk the letter-of-the-week approach once and for all. Teaching a letter a week means that children will not have learned the complete alphabet until sometime in March. Everything we have discussed so far related to children's learning indicates this is a dangerous idea:
  - They need repeated, varied exposure and practice with each individual letter over time (not all in one week).
  - Different children come to prekindergarten or kindergarten knowing different letters.
  - Although knowing the alphabet is essential to early literacy, there are numerous other essential language and literacy skills that must be taught, as well as critical content knowledge that must be developed (Teale, Paciga, and Hoffman 2010).

Teaching a different letter each week, no matter the order, is at best a waste of many children's time and can disadvantage children who depend heavily on school experiences for their early literacy learning.

Some effective alphabet knowledge approaches ramp up the pace considerably. As mentioned previously, Jones and colleagues (Jones, Clark, and Reutzel 2012), for example, teach one letter per day, thus allowing for up to seven possible alphabet knowledge review cycles over the course of the school year. Taking into consideration the Common Core State Standards that have as end-of-kindergarten expectations that children not only recognize and name all upper- and lowercase letters but also "Demonstrate basic knowledge of one-to-one letter–sound correspondences by producing the primary or many of the most frequent sounds for each consonant" and "Associate the long and short sounds with common spellings (graphemes) for the five major vowels," it seems obvious that foundational alphabet skills need to happen much sooner than any letter of the week program would provide.

- *Children who need extra support.* There are always a small number of children who, despite experiencing evidence-based classroom instruction and receiving additional individual support (Tier 2 instruction, for example), still have difficulty with some letters/ sounds. These children benefit from specialized, individual instruction provided outside the regular classroom program. Approaches of the sort researched by Brookfield et al. (2013) and Lafferty, Gray, and Wilcox (2005) have been shown to be effective. An important point with respect to these children and the instruction they receive is that the time they spend learning the alphabet should be no more than necessary, thus minimizing the number of things they miss in the regular curriculum. For example, Brookfield et al. (2013), working with individual children or pairs of children in sessions of two and a half to four minutes for an average of thirteen sessions, were able to help these children master troublesome letters.

  Another evidence-based approach for children who need Tier 3 instruction is the Interactive Strategies Approach (Scanlon, Anderson, and Sweeney 2011). Interactive Strategies Approach is designed primarily to accelerate the progress of primary-grade struggling readers in the areas of comprehension and foundational literacy skills. It focuses on increased motivation, knowledge of the alphabetic code, vocabulary, and comprehension, while also attending to young children's phonemic awareness and knowledge of conventions of print.

- *Other practices worth considering.* In addition to the instructional practices directly related to developing alphabet knowledge that have research backing, it is important to point out that other evidenced-based early childhood practices will contribute to young children's knowledge of print and alphabetic principles:

  - *Print-rich classroom literacy environments.* Print-rich classrooms deliberately employ various types of purposeful print in many areas of the room that is used by teachers and

For examples of how to fulfill each of these principles in practice

see Section 3

children as integral parts of numerous activities. Examples include sign-up sheets for centers, directions for how to complete small-group or independent center activities, and information about daily events in the classroom (schedule, what's for lunch, special guests, etc.). Such print resources change on a regular basis to reflect changing activities and children's skill levels. See Vukelich and Christie (2009) for many more examples.

- *High-quality, print-focused read-alouds.* The teacher uses a print-referencing style when conducting certain whole-class read-alouds to accelerate children's print knowledge development. In such read-alouds the teacher gives systematic attention to the print in the book through verbal and nonverbal references (Justice et al. 2010).

- *Interactive writing experiences.* A series of small-group lessons that create "contextualized instruction" by integrating explicit explanations, demonstrations, and phonological awareness/alphabet skills work into a connected series of activities that include a read-aloud, group writing in response to the text shared in the read-aloud, and word building (Craig 2006).

These instructional activities can be profitably incorporated into any early childhood classroom to promote a variety of aspects of early literacy learning, including alphabet knowledge.

Conclusion

I hope this section has helped you to see that alphabet knowledge—learning about letters and the sounds associated with them—is an indispensable part of early literacy development. I also hope that it has helped you understand that there is far more that young children need to learn beyond alphabet knowledge to be successful readers and writers in elementary school, secondary school, and beyond. That said, I want to stress another point that comes through strongly from the research: during preschool, kindergarten, and the first part of grade 1, it is important that children develop robust knowledge of letters and letter sounds. That is because another thing clearly indicated by research is that getting off to a good start with respect to the foundational skill of alphabet knowledge is critical: children who have not grasped phonological awareness and alphabet knowledge by the end of first grade are much more likely to experience continuing difficulties in reading and writing development (Juel 1988; Juel, Griffin, and Gough 1986).

The research also unequivocally indicates that no one program for teaching the alphabet is effective in all settings—there is no silver bullet. However, the traditional letter-of-the-week approach still common in many early childhood classrooms is not supported by empirical evidence. Teachers should abandon this practice in favor of instruction built on features discussed above that research does show are associated with learning the alphabet effectively. The following section applies the findings of this research to instruction in real classrooms.

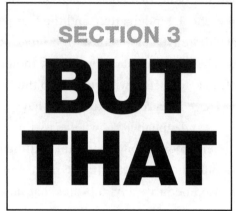

Inviting Children to Communicate Through Print

REBECCA McKAY

This section shares teaching strategies and routines based on research revealing how children learn the alphabet most effectively. These teaching recommendations are by no means exhaustive. As you live alongside children in your classroom, you will create many more, in many contexts, on your own. That's as it should be. Children learn best when alphabet learning happens in genuinely engaging contexts. Perhaps more importantly, when we invite children into the world of literacy, we help them imagine and create an identity through print (see Figure 3–1).

For children to develop knowledge of the alphabet, it's important to remember that they will need both explicit teaching and ample opportunities to practice using their growing letter–sound knowledge in authentic contexts. In the classroom, the relationship between explicit

Why is observation such an essential tool for teaching alphabet knowledge?

see Section 2, page 12, for information on how children learn to recognize the sounds and shapes of letters differently teaching and practice is quite fluid. As teachers interact with children who are writing independently across the day, they will see many opportunities to offer explicit teaching in the specific context of a child's writing. For example, if a teacher observes a child sounding out the word *circus*, she can use that as an opportunity to show the student that *c* can make different sounds—sometimes in the same word! Likewise, as a teacher explicitly demonstrates an alphabetic principle during a whole-class lesson, he may invite children to actively practice with him, thinking of what letter makes the sound at the beginning of *jam*, for instance, and which children in the room have names that start with this same sound (Jarod, Jaquon). The following strategies represent this fluid mix of explicit teaching and authentic practice.

Figure 3–1   How Print Informs a Child's Identity

Literacy Self-Concept	Strategies That Develop It
I can do things myself because of print.	Labeling Inquiry Signing in Self-initiated writing
I can anticipate/plan for what comes next because of print.	Morning meeting
I can communicate to make my wants and needs understood and to consider the wants and needs of others.	Morning meeting Signing in Inquiry
I can expand my understanding of the world and myself through print.	Reading aloud Interactive writing Student-authored class books Inquiry Integrated studies Self-initiated writing

(continues)

Figure 3–1 (contined)

Literacy Self-Concept	Strategies That Develop It
I can use print to hold on to information that is important to me.	Interactive writing: lists, predictable charts, class letters Inquiry Integrated studies Self-initiated writing
I can find joy in the aesthetics of language—the sound and feel of words, the patterns in a text, the rhythm of words and sentences, the levels of meaning a word can contain—and can see language as a tool for invention and play.	Manipulating props Name guessing game Movement game Singing songs Mixing up sentences Building words as a class Mind reading Interactive writing: predictable charts Self-initiated writing
I can use print to explain and describe the world and how it works.	Interactive writing: predictable charts, class books Inquiry Integrated studies
I can use print to solve problems.	Signing in Integrated studies Inquiry Self-initiated writing

Tracking Teaching over Time

One thing that can be hard when a teacher moves away from teaching a letter each week is losing that comfortable feeling of coverage. It takes a while to develop faith that you will actually be covering more when you embed your teaching of letters and sounds in authentic contexts throughout the day. Of course, you need more than faith; you also need a record of your teaching and your students' learning. And because you will often plan to teach a lesson on letters and sounds but won't know until after it's happened what information you actually talked about, sometimes the record will have to be made after you've engaged in inquiry with children instead of before.

As Bill explained in Section 2, there is no one ideal sequence of instruction, but it is worthwhile to plan with an understanding of what is easier and more difficult for most students. We can make some instructional decisions based on the following indicators that make some letters easier to learn:

- the letters appear in the student's name
- letters with regular letter–sound relationships
- high-frequency letters
- consonants that have the letter sound at the beginning or end of the letter name
- letters with distinctive visual features
- earlier letters in the alphabet.

To track individual students' alphabet knowledge and phonological awareness, see Figures 3–2 and 3–3.

I've included a sequence for tracking student learning with the letters presented according to the difficulty of learning (rather than alphabetical sequence). As Bill explained in Section 2, to increase children's flexibility in thinking about letters and their associated sounds, our weekly instruction should vary emphasis and sequence. The more challenging a letter, the greater the need for repeated instruction and practice.

Figure 3–2 Tracking Alphabet Knowledge

Alphabet Knowledge

Student Name: _____

CCSS.ELA-LITERACY.RF.K.1.D

Recognize and name all upper- and lowercase letters of the alphabet.

Check (✓) indicates mastery. **Boldface** indicates consonants with no letter name–letter sound association.

Most Frequently to Least Frequently Used Consonants		Capital		Lowercase	
R					
T					
N					
S					
L					
C (hard sound)	C (soft sound)	(hard)	(soft)	(hard)	(soft)
D					
P					
M					
B					
F					
V					
G (hard sound)	G (soft sound)	(hard)	(soft)	(hard)	(soft)
H					
K					
W					
X					
Z					
J					
Q					
Y					

Most Frequently to Least Frequently Used Vowels	Long Sound	Short Sound	Capital	Lowercase
I				
A				
E				
O				
U				

Figure 3–3 Tracking Phonological Awareness

Phonological Awareness

Student Name: _____

Standard	Taught	Mastered
CCSS.ELA-LITERACY.RF.K.2 Demonstrate understanding of spoken words, syllables, and sounds (phonemes).		
CCSS.ELA-LITERACY.RF.K.2.A Recognize and produce rhyming words.		
CCSS.ELA-LITERACY.RF.K.2.B Count, pronounce, blend, and segment syllables in spoken words.		
CCSS.ELA-LITERACY.RF.K.2.C Blend and segment onsets and rimes of single-syllable spoken words.		
CCSS.ELA-LITERACY.RF.K.2.D Isolate and pronounce the initial, medial vowel, and final sounds (phonemes) in three-phoneme (consonant-vowel-consonant, or CVC) words. (This does not include CVCs ending with /l/, /r/, or /x/.)		
CCSS.ELA-LITERACY.RF.K.2.E Add or substitute individual sounds (phonemes) in simple, one-syllable words to make new words.		

CCSS: www.corestandards.org/ELA-Literacy/RF/K/

We also keep in mind Bill's advice that our pacing should "emphasize teaching letters early and intensely and to the degree needed by each individual child." Although you gain a tremendous amount of insight into individual children's developing alphabet knowledge in informal interactions, you will also periodically need to assess their development more formally. You'll need records of both informal and formal assessments for each child. These assessments will help you work more thoughtfully with individual children, plan whole-class instruction to meet the broadest possible needs, and form small groups for more targeted instruction. With that need for differentiation in mind, you'll probably want to consider keeping separate records of your whole-class, small-group, and individual teaching. Beside each date for whole-class records, small-group list, or individual child's name, make notes about the information you shared in each teaching session. You might also make a grid with individual letters, blends, onsets, and so on that you know you need to cover so you can easily see if and when you've yet addressed all the aspects of developing letter knowledge that need to be covered.

In addition to whatever formal and informal assessment protocol your school suggests, it can be very helpful to simply sit down with each child every so often and ask her to go through and name the letters, letter sounds, blends, digraphs, etc., depending on what you are teaching. Using a simple grid that includes each letter and a column for name and sound, you can very quickly check off which letters and sounds a student has mastered and which she still needs support with. Because your alphabet teaching is embedded and contextualized, and because each of your students learns differently, you are likely to find both a lot of overlap in what students know and a lot of variation as well. Doing this kind of quick, informal letter–sound check a few times over the course of a season can be an invaluable way to keep track of students' growth over time and also to determine gaps in your teaching and to discover students who would benefit from small-group support focusing on the same letters or sounds.

Creating a Print-Rich Environment

For children to develop knowledge of the alphabet, it's important that they are immersed in a print-rich environment where they see all around them letters and sounds make words that do important work. Like many teachers, you may begin the year with very little on the walls of your classroom so students can contribute their ideas about how to decorate the space. However, you can still fill the room with environmental print that helps you and your students manage your space and your work and also builds a sense of community as you get to know each other. Because children will interact with this environmental print every day in meaningful ways, these words will become some of the first words many of them can read independently. For this reason, they are critical markers on the journey to developing alphabet knowledge because having known words to connect to unknown words is critical to development. After all, seeing the word *lunch* every day when children sign up for meal choices will help a lot as they come to own the *l* sound and the spelling of -*unch* (*munch, crunch, bunch*).

Creating a print-rich environment does not mean overloading your classroom with print. Too much print can be overwhelming and can in fact create the opposite of the intended effect. If your room is packed with charts that are loaded with text, students will have a hard time noticing the particular things you want them to notice. For that reason, it is important to choose environmental print thoughtfully and judiciously.

There are three main kinds of environmental print you can consider including in a classroom filled with young children: labels for objects and materials and spaces, labels for children's personal possessions, and all manner of lists that help manage your day to day work together.

Object, Material, and Space Labels

When young children enter preschool and kindergarten, they are surrounded by a world of new materials to explore and use. It takes time and scaffolding for children to learn to manage these materials independently, and labels serve an important function in that scaffolding while also creating a rich tableau of purposeful environmental print. Consider labeling relevant objects and materials in the classroom with a photograph and the corresponding written word. You may wonder why you would need a photograph of a pencil sharpener on the label that's stuck to the pencil sharpener itself. The answer lies in symbols. Even if children have limited print awareness when they begin school, they can match a physical item to its photograph, and it's exciting to watch students begin to use what they are learning about visual symbols to make a connection to print. They soon recognize that the word *scissors*, which at first may seem a series of unrelated letters, is, like the photograph of scissors, a symbol for the pair of scissors they are trying to retrieve or return to a spot on the shelf. As the year progresses, make sure cards, markers, and tape are available and encourage students to create labels of their own as they create, build, explore, and play throughout the day.

Name Labels

Children's names are another highly engaging source of purposeful environmental print, and as soon as students walk through the door on the first day of school, they can begin laying claim to their territory by placing their names on what is theirs: cubbies, book bags, self-portraits, and so on. To reinforce the connection between children and their written names, you might prepare name cards that include a small photograph (see Figure 3–4). Even children who cannot yet recognize their own name in print can identify their materials via their photograph, and the photographs help everyone connect names to faces.

Lists

All kinds of activities during the day might be managed by having children sign their names to lists and also to make lists for their own projects, explorations, and play. In addition to practice in writing their names and

Figure 3–4 Jack's Name Card

reading other children's names, the list itself and any choices it might contain have environmental print for children to read purposefully. Consider, for example, having lists around the room where children:

- show they have arrived at school
- indicate their choices from a lunch menu
- sign up for the centers they'd like to explore
- check out books from a class library.

You might also consider showing children how to use lists to solve problems and manage their work and play. Lists that track turn taking, for example, can tap into young children's need to manage fairness. A list of supplies needed to make a snack shows how notes help people remember. A list of the steps for cleaning the hamster cage shows how directions work. Luke created the list you see in Figure 3–5 during a transportation study when many children wanted to help paint the bike lane on the floor in the block area. The list effectively split the work up evenly among the children who wanted a turn.

Figure 3–5 Student-Created List for Turn-Taking

(6) KIS Tht SAD No	
Alejandro	No
Alex Moon	Yes
Alex Rubin	res
David	Yes
Floyd	No
Grainne	No
Jack	Yes
Jacob	Yes
Jola	Yes
Josephine	Yes
Luke	res
Maia	No
Nadav	yes
Noe	No
Olivia	Yes
Oren	Yes
Roman	Yes
Sienna	res
Sophie	No
Sydney	res
Talia	Yes
Will	

Luke wanted to know how many kids wanted to paint the bike lane in the block area.

15 KIS Tht SAD Yes

The point is, a list is an incredibly versatile tool that beginning readers and writers can easily use to help them understand the amazingly functional power of print to help people manage their everyday lives.

In addition to the three types of environmental print described here, you will undoubtedly be creating charts, both curriculum-related and non-curriculum-related, across the year. Classroom charts are another important source of environmental print. Particularly in pre-K and kindergarten classrooms, it is important to keep these charts simple—make use of symbols and pictures and other visual supports, and choose text that is familiar and meaningful to students. (See Martinelli and Mraz [2012] for many ideas about creating and using classroom charts.)

Drawing Attention to Print

A print-rich environment is critical, but by itself it's simply a context. How you live and learn with children inside that context is what really matters. You have to show children how to interact with the print around them in ways that will develop their knowledge of the alphabet. Whether you're reading aloud to the whole class, working with a small group, or engaged in countless other activities during the day, opportunities to draw children's attention to letters and sounds abound. The key is to recognize the need for this in developing children's alphabet knowledge; look for logical opportunities to draw attention to letters and sounds, and then embed this teaching seamlessly into the day.

Without question, the most obvious context for drawing children's attention to print is when you share books with them during read-alouds. (For a list of books, see Appendix A.) Imagine, for example, reading the title of Mo Willems' *Don't Let the Pigeon Drive the Bus!* (2003) and simply pointing out that *pigeon* starts with a *p*, /p/, just as *penguin* did in the book you read last week. You might even quickly write each word (or just the letter)

> **For the research that supports teaching alphabet knowledge through read-aloud**
>
> see Section 2, page 30

on a whiteboard so children can see them. Using alphabet knowledge to figure out words can also be demonstrated during a read-aloud session. For instance, you might look for a situation in which a word could, from the picture and context, be either *dog* or *puppy* and then have children help you look at the letters in the word to figure out which it is.

The key to using read-aloud successfully as a context for drawing children's attention to print is to not overdo it so it gets in the way of meaning. You might consider revisiting books over time so children have multiple experiences to make meaning and also learn from the rich print demonstrations offered by the text.

Read-aloud is not the only opportunity for drawing children's attention to print, however. Basically any time you are with children and there is print around, you might decide to call attention to it. Imagine you're looking at books with a small group of children in the science center and you read a label on a picture of a mosquito. You stop to marvel at the sound of the word and its spelling. "I just love the way this word sounds. *Mosquito. M-o-s-q-u-i-t-o,*" you say, pointing to each letter in the word. Or perhaps a student, Charlie, is the helper for the day, his name prominently displayed on the agenda chart. You take time to consider the *ch* at the beginning of his name and other words that have those letters and that sound in them too. Or perhaps you are walking your students to the cafeteria and they notice the illuminated exit sign—you might pause to draw students' attention to the letters in *exit*, and think together about other words that have the letter *x* in them. The possibilities are endless!

Making connections like these and drawing children's attention to letters and sounds serve as important demonstrations of an attentive stance to print, while also providing an opportunity for explicit teaching. And when children see you attending in this way, their interest is piqued and they are likely to offer their own questions and observations about letters and sounds and how spellings work. Anytime they do, of course, be sure to tap into their interest and take the opportunity to do some explicit teaching to support it.

Manipulating Props

As another way to draw children's attention to print, you might occasionally set the stage to encourage experiences with a particular letter as children explore and play throughout the day. For instance, if you are talking about the letter *b* in morning meeting or some other context, you might add a butterfly net and butterflies to the pretend play area—or bagels, along with buttons the kids can use as money to buy them. In the writing center, consider adding objects (or stencils of objects) that begin with the letter *b* to stimulate independent writing that supports earlier work. Don't be surprised when students proudly announce their discoveries ("Hey! *Butterfly* begins with *b*!") and use the stencils to draw bears and bugs labeled with *b*'s. When the objects are discovered by students, try to make sure you are out and about, ready to teach into their discoveries as they make them.

Reading and Writing the Morning Message

Most classrooms have some sort of whole-class morning gathering where everyone meets to greet one another and think about the day ahead. Because this time is predictable and routine, and because it includes communicating important information, it's the perfect context in which to embed some explicit teaching about the alphabet target letters and sounds children have not yet mastered and connect to whatever messages you have to convey. There are many ways this teaching might happen, depending on your specific routines, priorities, and teaching style. To help you imagine what this teaching might look like, I offer one example of a systematic approach to crafting a morning message that includes explicit teaching of alphabet knowledge and concepts of print. You can help students read the message at the beginning of the morning meeting, but no doubt, with daily practice, they will quickly be able to decode most of it on their own (or collaboratively with their peers).

Using this structure, you prepare each morning message so that it has three parts, separated into three lines and embedded with different supports. The first line, always written in red, is a greeting. This line is used to explore initial sounds and one-to-one correspondence. For instance, if the greeting says "Yo" and a student reads it as "Hello," you draw her attention to the initial sound and to check whether it's a match. If she reads it accurately, you can talk about how someone might figure the word out, if they were stumped. If the first line reads "Good morning" and a student reads it as "Hi," you can explore one-to-one correspondence. "Let's see how many words *Hi* is. Count with your fists. *Hi.* Let's double-check. *Hi.* Yep, it's only one word, and it sounds like a short word too. Now let's count how many words are in the red line. Count while I touch the words. One, two. Yes, it's two words. *Hi* is not a match. Let's try something else." Similarly, if the child reads the greeting accurately, you can still use this as an opportunity to count the words.

The second line, written in blue, reinforces patterns, which are an integral part of the earliest levels of children's books. At first the pattern is simple, three words that remain consistent over time: "Today is [day name]." Students quickly realize that the first two words in this line will always be *today* and *is* and then use decoding strategies—such as the initial sound or background knowledge—to figure out the third word, the day of the week ("I know it says *Monday*, because I go to dance on Mondays and my mom said I'm going to dance after school today"). When most students clearly no longer need supports to read the sentence pattern, you can change to a different pattern and explore it over time. For example, "The weather today is _____" or "This is the _____ day of the week." Any sentence will really do, as it's the repetition of the pattern that provides the scaffold.

Depending on your needs, you can use the third black line as an opportunity to do different kinds of meaning work: make an announcement, share some news, name a goal for the day, ask a question to launch a discussion. It really doesn't matter what it communicates because the teaching you do with this line is more variable and depends on the words the message contains. This is the content-rich part of the message for children, but what also matters is that you are also intentional about taking time to talk about letters and sounds in conjunction with it. For example, you might stop to notice and name the letters in a whole word or the letters that make up a particular part of a word. You might make connections between the letters and sounds in an unknown word with a word or words more familiar to the children. You might marvel at an unexpected spelling, like the *sch* in *school*. You might ask the children which word they'd like to talk about and then build your teaching from there. Be sure to have a whiteboard or iPad handy, as you will often be thinking aloud with the children about other letters and sounds and words and it helps to write them so children can see them.

You might, at times, incorporate the tools of interactive writing (see the following section) into the morning message, for example, leaving out a word and asking children to figure out what the missing word should be. As the year progresses, you might ask students to compose the morning messages, as Aisha is doing in Figure 3–6. Students might also lead a conversation about some aspect of alphabet knowledge that intrigues them in their message, with you at the ready to provide support and accurate, explicit information.

Figure 3–6 Aisha Contributes a Morning Message

Interactive Writing

Interactive (or shared) writing is a common practice in many early childhood classrooms and it's another smart context in which to embed explicit teaching about the alphabet and a host of other concepts of print, as well as demonstrate the kinds of thinking writers do as they compose text. Interactive writing is a collaborative endeavor where children—as a whole class, in small groups, or individually—work with a teacher to compose a text from start to finish while sharing their strategic thinking throughout the process.

> **The stretching of words and identification of sounds within words involves phonological awareness**
>
> see page 13 for research on that topic

Although a great deal of information about letters and sounds is shared in interactive writing, the focus is on strategically *using* this information to spell words. To this end, you'll want to prompt children to stretch out words orally, identify sounds, and figure out which letters might make those sounds. When you engage students in this way, you'll see a range of natural development. Some students may only be able to hear and identify one sound in a word, others can identify several, and some students will know how to write the word conventionally without even sounding it out. Be sure to validate all levels of understanding so children know you value their participation, not perfection.

Depending on what you're writing and the needs of your students, you might also describe the formation of letters that are challenging to write, remind children of spelling patterns that don't match their sounds (like a plural *s*, which often sounds like a *z* at the end of a word), or point them to classroom resources that can support them as they spell (the word wall, for example).

As a teaching strategy, interactive writing can be used across the day for many different purposes, and it seems children attend to it more intentionally when it has some purpose beyond the act of writing itself. For this reason, you'll want to look for opportunities to create really meaningful texts in your interactive writing lessons. Next, I highlight three specific ways you might use this strategy in your classroom, but know that the possibilities are really endless as you imagine this same kind of work in your own classroom.

Shared Experiences, Class Letters, and Predictable Charts

Shared experiences make particularly good topics for interactive writing, as children generally have lots to contribute and are excited to see their ideas put into words they can read. If your class goes on a field trip, has an interesting visitor, or attends some event at school, consider creating a text through interactive writing about your experience. Also, be on the lookout for those unexpected moments that happen in the natural course of the day. A sudden thunderstorm that draws everyone to the window. A particularly fun time preparing snack together. A really funny mishap in the blocks center. Interactive writing provides a way to share these experiences with families and school personnel who weren't present for them. They make great topics for interactive writing, can be written in a variety of genres, and the words connected to them are often rich with possibilities for thinking about letters and sounds as you write them. Keep in mind that writing about these experiences can be a good opportunity for creating "multimodal" texts that use both pictures and words. For example, you or one of the children can take a digital photo of that thunderstorm and include it in the final version along with the written text the children have created.

Interactive writing can also be used to collaboratively compose texts that do important work for your classroom community. Writing letters and sending them through personal delivery (to the principal or another classroom), through the mail, or electronically is a good example. Because written letters have a specific purpose and audience, and because they present the clear promise of a response, children are often very invested in them and very intentional about the messages they convey. For example, if you are engaged in an inquiry of some kind and you have a question that needs answering, consider composing a letter, email, or tweet together through interactive writing and sending it to a person you suspect might have an answer. If you find you need something for your classroom, a letter might just do the trick. You might write letters of invitation, gratitude, condolences—any of the real-world reasons people write them! Be aware that often a class letter is too long to compose in one interactive writing session, so you might need to revisit it over time. Figure 3–7 is an invitation to a publishing party from one kindergarten class to another.

Figure 3–7 Letter Inviting Another Class to Publishing Party

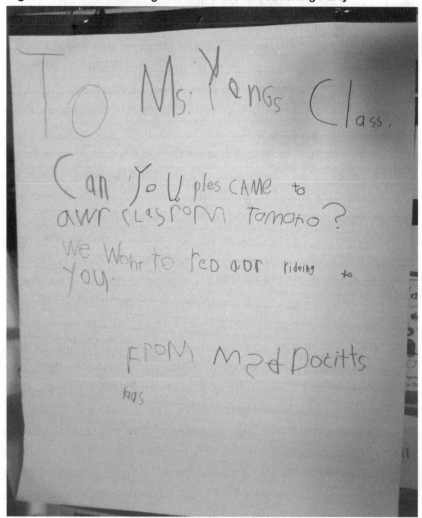

Finally, consider using interactive writing to make predictable charts about all kinds of topics across the curriculum that interest the children and you. These charts have simple patterns that repeat, only one or two words changing in each line (similar to guided reading books at levels A and B), so they are great for helping students use their emergent reading skills. Imagine, for example, charts with patterns like these:

- Outside the window I see _____.
- In my family, we _____ together.
- A good scientist _____.

The possibilities are really limitless. These types of charts are a bit different from teacher-designed curricular charts described earlier in the environmental print section. These charts may indeed focus on some element of the curriculum, or they may arise spontaneously from classroom conversation or other experiences. Either way, the predictable pattern and use of high-frequency words are key. When a chart is complete, often after more than one session of interactive writing, you might turn it into a class book, put it in the classroom library, and add small copies of it to students' independent reading book bins. These kinds of books are often the most popular of all!

To really draw children's attention to letters and sounds right from the start, your first predictable chart could be an alphabet chart. If it is, then both the making of the chart (through interactive writing) and the topic of the chart itself will support children's growing knowledge of the alphabet. To keep it simple, you might ask students to identify items in your classroom that begin with each letter of the alphabet. Tackle a few letters at a time over a period of several days: "*A* is for _____. *B* is for _____. *C* is for _____," and so on. As kids come up with ideas, add them to the chart and draw students' attention to initial, ending, or medial sounds in each word as you write it. "*Folders.* F-f-f-folders. What sound do you hear at the beginning of *folders?* What letter goes with the /f/ sound? Yes, *f.* Who thinks they can find the word *folders* in this line? How did you know that was *folders*? Yes, this word begins with *f*. It is *folders*."

Self-Initiated Writing

Perhaps the most important way children come to understand the remarkable power of literacy to help them construct identity is by becoming authors who write about their interests, share their stories or information, and imagine new worlds with words. Providing time, space, and materials for children to do what authors (and illustrators) do and make books of their own is therefore essential. Children become known by the topics they choose to write about: Alexis loves to write about cats. Jamal is a dinosaur expert.

The self-initiated writing children do when they make their own books is where the rubber meets the road. All the other activities we plan to help them learn the alphabet and develop phonological awareness mean nothing unless the end result is that children use their growing knowledge to make meaning. Children need a daily chance to do the challenging thinking involved in figuring out how to say what they want to say. Demonstrated time and again in interactive writing, basic spelling strategies help children make use of all they're learning throughout the day:

- "Is this a word you've written so many times you don't even have to think about how it's spelled, you just know it?"
- "Have you ever seen this word? Can you picture the letters in it?"
- "Is this word anything like another word you know how to spell?"

Breaking a word apart into sounds involves phonemic segmentation

see Section 2, page 13

- "Say the word slowly. What sounds do you hear at the beginning? What letter or letters can we use for that sound?"
- "Say the word slowly again. What is the next sound you hear? What letter or letters can we use for that sound?"
- And so on until the last sound in the word and the letter or letters to represent that sound.

Looking closely at children's self-initiated writing is the best assessment tool for whether they can use their growing knowledge base to actually do what it's intended to do—write words that make meaning. Phonemic awareness and alphabet knowledge assessments are essential for understanding student difficulty, like distinguishing between a phonemic segmentation issue and a letter–sound knowledge issue. Through self-initiated writing, we are able to see what information children have at their disposal to help them figure out the spellings for all kinds of words. It's the perfect time to pull up a chair and work one-on-one with a student because you can match your teaching directly to that child's needs. You can also point out the strategies children use successfully as they puzzle out the many workings of print. As you assess children's development over time, the goal is for them to make better and better spelling approximations as their knowledge grows through both experience and your explicit teaching. And as they also grow as readers, their writing will begin to show more conventional spellings for words they've encountered many times in print.

For self-initiated writing to pay off in these ways, children need to feel comfortable taking risks. Beginning writers have heard and spoken thousands and thousands of words they don't recognize in print and certainly don't know how to spell. If Jamal wants to draw on his rich knowledge of dinosaurs, for example, he can't be afraid to try spelling *Tyrannosaurus rex* or *meteors*. Even very common words can seem risky to children trying to spell them for the first time. These simple practices encourage children to take risks:

- In interactive writing, show children how to use strategies to generate spellings and have them help you decide which letters to use. The point is not to come up with a conventional spelling but a *strategic* one.

For more on how children's misspellings give you important information about their alphabet knowledge

see Section 2, page 16

- Celebrate their attempts to spell challenging words. Put the attempts on charts for everyone to see, and let the children who tried them explain their thinking.
- Read children's books to the whole class so everyone can hear rich language in context.
- Discuss why approximation is necessary—they know so many words, they can't possibly be expected to know how to spell them all. Assure them that even the most experienced writers don't know how to spell every single word they know.
- Most importantly, don't correct children's writing. Letting approximations stand shows you value children's best efforts. Beginning writers aren't approximating because they're being careless or not trying hard enough. They are using everything they know to generate the spellings we see. As they grow into themselves as writers, you will find opportunities to teach spelling and conventions, but especially early on, think of students' writing approximations as a window into what they know rather than call out all that they don't know. As you read in Part 2, research supports providing children many opportunities to spell words based on the sounds they hear, rather than just directing them to the conventional spelling.

Students Publish in the Classroom Library

A natural outgrowth of self-initiated writing is that students love to write, illustrate, and publish their own books. Displaying their work alongside professionally published books in your classroom library reinforces the idea that their written words and images are powerful and carry messages meant to be read by others. Students need to experience personally the power writing can hold to develop a positive connection to writing. You might wonder how placing books children have created in the classroom library helps them build knowledge of the alphabet, especially when these books are filled with all sorts of wonderful approximations of how letters and sounds work. The answer is simple, really. When children see themselves as writers and illustrators and really come to own that identity, the *need* to know how letters and sounds work—and all kinds of other skills and strategies for writing—is much more pressing (in a good way, of course).

Creating Class Books to Support Alphabet Knowledge

Sometimes a whole class can work together to make a book, each child contributing one or several pages. Don't be surprised if these books become the most worn and well-loved books in your classroom library (see Figure 3–8). Familiar with their content, emergent readers approach these books with a sense of ownership and find success with

Figure 3–8   Students Reading Class Book

them because they often have predictable patterns and contain their own and their classmates' names. During the year, you might make all kinds of collaborative books, but early in the year consider book projects designed to specifically build children's alphabet knowledge. Here are two possibilities.

The Letter–Shape Book. Touching and seeing things can help children learn; this book project gives them a chance to explore the shapes of letters visually and kinesthetically. Working with three children at a time, explain that you're going to make a book like the ABC books in your library that have one letter on each page, but that your book will be special because the children are going to be in it. Each of them is going to use their classmates' bodies to form a letter of the alphabet.

Give each child a choice of three letters you know he or she still needs support in learning. Together, let the students identify the distinctive features of their letter. For instance, a capital *R* has one straight long vertical or up-and-down line, one small curve at the top, and one little diagonal line from the middle to the bottom. When the student is ready, she forms the letter by having classmates lie on the ground in the appropriate formation. Take a picture from above and let the child who's responsible for the letter review it. If she wants to make changes, she can. Then move on to the next child and the next letter. If the student needs extra support, you can tape an outline on the rug as a guide.

Students love using their bodies in this way, and the project heightens their awareness of the shapes and features of letters. When all the letters have been formed and photographed, to create a paper book, place a sheet of acetate on top of each photograph and form an outline of the letter in permanent marker, then bind the photographs together into a book. Or, assemble the photographs digitally and publish an online book, placed in a secure area of your classroom website for children to share with their families at home.

The Letter–Sound Book. To support a growing knowledge of the sounds each letter makes, consider creating an alphabet book featuring letters and their sounds (see Figure 3–9). There are several ways this might happen. You might assign each child a letter of the alphabet (or let the children choose one). Then, working in pairs, have children find things in the classroom (or school) that begin with their letter and a sound commonly represented by the letter and photograph them. Even

Figure 3–9   Student-Created Page for the Letter *K*

though each child is working on an individual letter sound, having another student along on the search gives opportunities to share their thoughts and learn from each other's discoveries. You might go as a class on a walk and find things to photograph outside that could represent different letter sounds, or have children bring photos from home.

Why is it so important to distinguish instruction in this way?

see Section 2, page 27

Alternatively, children can illustrate (instead of photograph) a page for a specific letter, drawing and labeling the objects that contain the letter sound. In either case, you will want to work with children to ensure that the objects represented really go with the letter. For example, *knee* sounds like it goes on the *N* page, and you will have to explain why it doesn't. It is also important to strive to represent both of the most common sounds represented by each of the vowels and by *c* and *g* to develop children's knowledge of each of these important sound–letter relationships. However you decide to create a book of letter sounds, the important thing is that children are thinking about the words that name different objects and the sounds that make up those words.

Inquiry

Inquiry is a very valuable framework for threading literacy, math, science, and social studies curricula together. Truly, anything children show a deep interest in can become an inquiry—from windmills to neighborhood murals to grocery stores to falling autumn leaves. When children are deeply engaged in authentic inquiries, their research creates a pressing need for reading and writing, and hence, the alphabet knowledge that makes both possible. Additionally, the vocabulary connected to different topics of inquiry is often rich and varied, and children's attention to and interest in these new words is heightened. For these reasons, engaging classroom inquiry is one of the best contexts in which to grow children's alphabet knowledge.

For example, consider a group of children who were intrigued by transportation. Notice all the ways a *need* for reading and writing was woven into their inquiry. With the street intersection outside their school as their focus, the children undertook a deep study of a topic that fascinated them (see Figures 3–10a and 3–10b). They brainstormed and tallied the different modes of transportation people use, made predictions about which modes of transportation are fastest or most efficient, and re-created the intersection outside their school in the classroom block area. They took a field trip to a woodworking shop where they created

Figure 3–10a   Student Hypotheses for Transportation Study

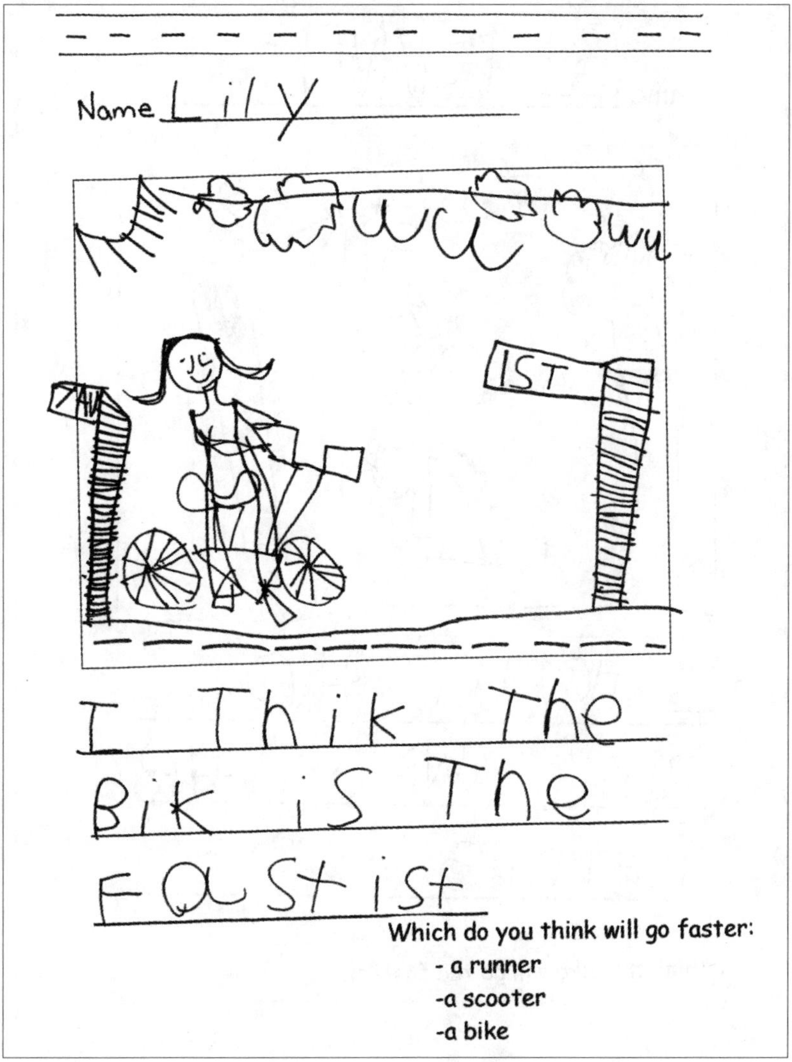

Name Lily

I Thik The Bik is The Foustist

Which do you think will go faster:
- a runner
- a scooter
- a bike

toy cars, and then they constructed an intersection on their playground where they could practice the rules of the road. Working together, students designed a driving test and issued drivers' licenses. Throughout the unit students wrote interactively and independently (personal narratives and nonfiction books as well as street signs), listened to their teacher read nonfiction aloud, and created predictable charts that were later turned into texts children could read on their own.

Figure 3–10b   Student Hypotheses for Transportation Study

I think the bike will go the fastest.

Learning About Letters and Sounds in Names, Songs, Poems, and Games

Developing phonological awareness and learning the alphabet go hand in hand. Fortunately, young children naturally savor delicious-sounding words and are eager to play with sounds in familiar words. Perhaps they are so attuned to sounds because that's what words first were for them, *sounds.* They came to understand language by listening and making sense of sound, and they're still close enough to that time in

> **What's the relationship between phonological awareness and graphophonic development?**
>
> see Section 2, page 9

their lives that their sense of sound is heightened. Children fall over laughing when the anxious mouse in Ruth Stiles Gannett's classic *My Father's Dragon* yells "Bome cack! Bome cack!" to the fleeing dragon. It *sounds* so funny to them. They listen on the edge of their seats to see what silly word work Ruth Stiles Gannett will use next.

As teachers, you can capitalize on the pleasure many young children take in the sound of words as you teach them the symbols that mix and mingle to represent those sounds in print. What follows is a menu of possibilities for exploring letters and sounds in children's names, in songs and poems, and in a variety of games children will enjoy playing as they're learning the alphabet and developing their phonological awareness.

Learning Through Children's Names

Because children's names are all over the room in various places for various reasons, and because children so easily associate the spoken names of their classmates with the written names (especially when photos are attached), the twenty or so names you find on your class list each year will become one of the first, most important re-

> **Children typically know the names of the letters in their names before the letter sounds, so it's a strong foundation to teach from**
>
> see Section 2, page 12

sources for information about letters and sounds. Obviously, you can't predict what alphabetic information you will find in a list of student names, but it's sure to be rich with possibility because names can be spelled in many different ways and have very different origins. Here are a few simple ideas for capitalizing on the rich storehouse of information offered by the names of your students.

Name Inquiry. Early in the year as children are getting to know one another, you might take a few minutes each day to study one child's name. You can select names randomly, or you might study your class list and plan the inquiries in a strategic order that will showcase more common alphabet information first and move to more sophisticated. When you study a child's name, first talk a little about where the name came from, whether it's a nickname or a given name, and any other interesting facts about the name. (It's important to be mindful that some children may not be comfortable with their names being discussed.) Next, turn your attention to the sounds in the name first, and then the letters. To build phonological awareness, first talk about the name without looking at it in print. You might consider the following questions:

- "Say the name slowly. What different sounds do you hear?"
- "Do you know any other names or words that sound similar?"
- "How many syllables (or some teachers use the term *beats*) are in the name?"

After you've explored the sound of the name a bit, then study it in print. You might consider:

- "What are the letters in the name?" (You might reveal them one at a time, modeling the formation of each one, or all at once.)
- "What are some of the shapes you see in these letters?" (Consider asking the child which letter is the most challenging to form.)

- "Which letters, alone or together, are making the different sounds in the name?"
- "Do you see any letters or letter combinations that you've seen in other names or words?"

After you have studied a child's name, be intentional about adding the alphabetic information that name offered to your explicit teaching throughout the day. For example, if a child is puzzling over the spelling of *frog* (perhaps struggling to hear both sounds in the blend *fr*), and you have a Francisco in the room, help the child make the connection between the *fr* in *Francisco* and the *fr* in *frog*.

Many teachers elaborate on this kind of name study by asking each student to draw a portrait and write the name of the student whose name has been studied. Portraits can be collected and stapled into a book, which then either remains in the classroom as a resource or goes home with the child. Some teachers also post names that have been studied either on the class word wall or elsewhere in the room so that students can refer to the names when they are writing.

Using Names During Transitions. When students are lining up to go to lunch or out to recess, consider using the letter and sound information in their names as a management tool for this routine. You might focus on letters. "If your name starts with a *P*, please join the line." Or, you might focus on sounds. "If your name ends with the ē sound, please join the line." Get as sophisticated as you like, depending on the development of your students. "If your name has an *i* and an *e* in it, side by side, please join the line." The point is to have children think about the letters and sounds in their names and their classmates' names and, over time, to be able to think about the names using only their memory and without looking at the print. You can also have children think of an answer to a question like "What is your favorite color?" and then you play the same sort of game with their answers. "If your favorite color starts with a *Y*, please join the line." Names can be used in this way for any routine that requires children to complete some action, so just imagine the possibilities throughout the day.

A Guessing Game with Names. Early in the year, you might make simple cards for the students on which their name is written next to their photograph. To begin the game, choose a name that begins with an uncommon letter (whenever possible, the only name in the class that begins with that letter). Show the students the name on the card while covering the image with your hand and ask, "Whose name is this?" Follow up students' answers with, "How do you know?" Most often it's a variation of "I know it's Sophie's name because Sophie's name starts with an *s*!"

If you ask other students for their opinions before revealing the image, you will almost certainly extend the potential of the embedded learning.

"I think it's Sophie, too!"

"How do you know?"

"Because /s/ goes with *s* and I see an *s*."

"So you agree? Let's look at the picture and double-check. Yes, it is Sophie's name!"

When students are ready for more, consider choosing a child's name that begins with the same letter as several other class members' names. If you hold up Aniya's name, someone might guess Ashlynn. Encourage the students to listen for the ending sound when you say Ashlynn's name, ask them to identify it, then prompt them to look at the ending of Aniya's name and see whether there's an *n* there. "Nope, it's not a match. Let's try something else."

Later in the year, when children know each other's names automatically, you might play this same game with words from your inquiries across the day in social studies, science, and math. Children who have a more developed understanding of letter sounds will likely be able to use the length of the word to inform their answers; identify and use medial sounds, blends, and digraphs; and recognize similarities between words (common spelling patterns and word families).

Making New Names. As children become familiar with both the sounds and letters in each other's names, you might play a game where you create a new class list of names you've invented by combining different parts of students' names in different ways. Take the *sh* from Shania's name, combine it with the *ederick* part of Frederick's name, and you have a new student on your list, *Shederick.* Christina and Sophia become *Chrophia* (consider how the *o* might change the way you say *Chr*) or even *Sostina.* Be sure to let students take the lead in imagining new combinations, and be sure to slow down and notice both how the new name looks and how it sounds. Children find this game hilarious and it really focuses their attention on oral segmenting and blending— listening to what happens when you take words apart and put them back together in a new way. And as with all the other name games, as the year moves on, consider playing the same game with other kinds of words you're encountering across the day—what happens when you mix up math and reading? *Meading* and *Rath!* Hilarious. And an engaging way to play with oral segmenting and blending.

Learning Through Songs and Poems

One of the joys of spending our days in classrooms with young children is the fact they are often filled with song. In addition to being joyful, singing supports students' oral language development, introduces new vocabulary, and gives children a chance to experience rhythm, rhyme, and pattern in language. Poetry, recited well and often, serves the same purpose. In many classrooms, familiar songs and poems are written out on large charts or made into books to support students' emergent reading in the context of shared reading. Shared reading can be an invaluable method, the full explanation of which is beyond the scope of this book. The International Literacy Association (reading .org) includes a number of resources related to this topic.

For now, let's examine songs and poems as the rich storehouses of alphabetic and phonological information they are. In addition to helping children become familiar with the written words in a song or poem, turning their attention to the *sounds* of the words is a wonderful way to strengthen phonological awareness. You might consider talking about the words and sounds of a familiar (even memorized) song or poem so that children focus solely on the sounds of the words without looking at the text. Children will undoubtedly notice rhyming words early on, but you can also draw their attention to alliteration or particular letter sounds or blends you are currently studying as a class. In addition to simply noticing, appreciating, and delighting in the sounds the poems or songs offer, you can take the opportunity to focus your students' attention on any particular sound or pattern that you wish for them to notice. You might ask, "Are there words in this song that sound the same? Why do you think that is? How would it change the song for this word to have a different sound?" After talking about what students hear, just as you do when you study children's names and other words, you might turn their attention to the print and notice how the words are written. It is fascinating to pay attention to how what students hear transfers (or doesn't) into what they notice about the written words— what you notice can often provide you with information about what to teach next! For a list of great songs and poems, see Appendix B.

Learning Through Games

Word games are a staple for many of us in our everyday lives. Whether it's a quick round of Scrabble on a smartphone or a leisurely morning with the crossword in our local paper, we like to play with words. Children will, too, if we plan games for them that are engaging while also doing the important work of teaching them about letters and sounds. Although hopefully all the different explorations you've read about so far have an air of playfulness about them, here are a few actual games designed to be equally fun and informative.

Building Words. A set of laminated cards, each containing one letter of the alphabet, can be used to play all sorts of games with children (it helps to have multiple cards of each letter so you can use them in different ways). One way to use the cards is to explore high-frequency words you want children to be able to spell conventionally. I'll use *can* as an example. In the meeting area, hand a letter (a *c*, an *a*, an *n*) to each student and challenge the student to find two classmates who have the letters the child needs to complete the word *can*. When students have put the puzzle together, another student can double-check that the word is spelled correctly.

In another game, children are given different, random letters (it helps to have multiple vowels and high-frequency consonants in the mix). The goal is for a group of children to be standing at the front of the meeting area with their cards displaying a conventionally spelled word. One child starts, let's say he has an *m*, and chooses another child to stand beside him. Let's say that child has an *a*. He then chooses another child to stand beside him who has a letter that will continue a logical word. This continues until the children believe they have made the longest word they can make with the available letters. The class evaluates the convention of the spelling and may suggest changes. If a child believes she has been added to the word and there is no way she will work in that place—a *k* after an initial *m*, for instance—she can choose a child to replace her in the word.

You can give every child a different letter and then have each move around to find other children with letters that will make words. If *d* can find *o* and *g*, for example, they line up and display their word. And for very young children, you might give them each a card and simply call them up by letters to show them how to make different words.

Once children are lined up with letter cards that form words, then you can play with them in all kinds of ways. For example, let's say seven students have cards that spell the word *unhappy*. You might ask the letters that spell the /p/ sound to step forward. Or the prefix *un-*, the letter or letters that make the /ē/ sound, the letters that make the middle syllable. And again, with very young children, you might simply ask the *a* to step forward. You can remove parts of words—two children step away and now we have *happy*—or you can add endings. The possibilities are really limitless.

Riddle Jumping. With masking tape and a little bit of space, you can easily create a game for small groups of children with similar learning needs. First, determine which letter names and sounds each child needs more exposure to. Then work with three students at a time who need to focus on the same four letters. As you introduce each letter, ask questions such as, "What do you know about this letter? What sound goes with this letter? Can you think of any words that begin with this letter? Does anyone in our class have a name that begins with this letter? Does anyone in our class have this letter in his or her name somewhere, maybe not at the beginning but in the middle or at the end?" Discuss where these letters occur and their distinctive features.

Next, have students place four small pieces of masking tape on the floor within jumping distance of one another and write one of the four letters on each piece of tape. It's helpful to have cards with the letters written on them for students who need a model to copy. Then the fun begins! Students jump to each letter using letter names, sounds, and familiar words that you provide as clues: "Jump to the letter that goes with the /p/ sound." "Jump to the letter that begins Pedro's name." "Jump to the letter that you hear at the end of Jeff's name." In their excitement, don't be surprised if children call out the answer as they jump. If you hold up index cards with the correct response, you reinforce the sound–print connection. Finally, you can let each child lead a round of the game by giving the clues.

Writing on the Walls. As Bill explained in Section 2, producing the letters helps children recognize them. Although not really a game, the spirit of this activity is so playful it makes sense to include it here. You can take advantage of the-bigger-the-better concept when you explore letter formation. Tape a large piece of chart paper on a smooth wall or door and outline a letter in crayon. One by one, students visit the wall and trace the letter, each with a different-color crayon (see Figure 3–11). They see *and* feel the shape of the letter and experience the physical motions needed to form it. Pushing hard and pulling the crayon down the surface in one big gesture gives them a jolt of sensory feedback, and the messiness of layering letter on top of letter is very appealing. You might have every child engage with this activity at the beginning of the year, or just small groups later on who are still working out letter formation in their development. In fact, using a variety of sensory materials (writing letters in shaving cream, on sandpaper, on Styrofoam, and so on) to practice letter learning can be engaging for all children, and it can provide the kind of sensory feedback that some children in particular benefit from when learning letter formation and making the connection between letter shape, letter name, and letter sound.

In this section, I've taken you through many facets of learning the alphabet. At this point, I hope you feel confident about why and how

Figure 3–11 Retracing the Letter *B*

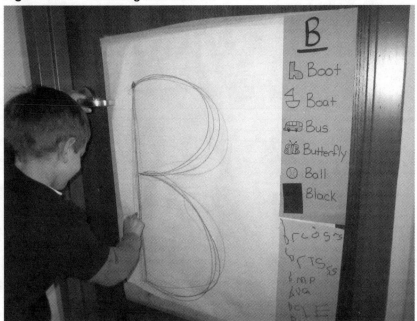

you can do better than letter-of-the-week. Together, Bill and I have shown you how joyful, meaningful, and effective letter work in the classroom can be. Put the macaroni and beans from your old letter-of-the-week instruction to good use—make a big pot of minestrone for yourself or for the local shelter. Put students' time to good use and make sure their alphabet learning focuses on the sounds, sense, and purpose of letters—to learn and communicate about the world.

AFTERWORD

NELL K. DUKE

One of the most difficult challenges you face as a teacher is to teach against the grain: to teach in a way that departs from how you were taught, how your mentor taught, how your friends and colleagues teach. And perhaps few instructional practices are as ingrained as teaching a letter a week. But you know now that in this case, teaching against the grain is the right thing to do. Teaching a letter of the week for twenty-six weeks is neither the most effective nor the most efficient and it's not the most compelling way to teach the alphabet to young children. You can do better—much better—and we hope that you can persuade your friends, colleagues, even your mentors to do better too.

I completely understand the insecurities that can come with moving away from a letter-a-week approach. I so appreciate the power of Bill Teale's review of research to convince us that this is the right thing to do. I so appreciate the confidence-building tools and techniques that Becky McKay shares. I love that Becky provides a tool to help us track which letters and sounds children have learned and which merit further attention. I love that Becky offers many ideas for structuring the curriculum such that it is more meaningful to students than a week on X and actually provides more opportunities for effective alphabet instruction.

As you well know, some children don't rely on us to develop their alphabet knowledge. Some come to us with deep knowledge of letters and sounds, perhaps even decoding words already. But as you also well know, some children depend almost entirely on us to learn the alphabet. Those children need and deserve for us to teach them letters and sounds, to develop their phonological awareness and print concepts, in the most powerful way we can find. If we're not confident that we've provided this essential foundation in letter–sound knowledge, phonological awareness, and print concepts, we risk setting a negative momentum for children's literacy: they may enter first grade lacking skills to make sense of new words; they may become reluctant readers who choose to avoid the difficulty of reading new texts; without strong reading lives, they may not gather the background knowledge and habits that will allow them future academic success. That's what can happen if we don't employ alternatives to letter-of-the-week.

Mark Twain once said, "Do the right thing. It will gratify some people and astonish the rest." As you move away from a letter a week, know that Becky, Bill, Ellin, and I will be gratified. And know that your colleagues may well be astonished—astonished at the depth with which you develop students' alphabet knowledge. Moving away from letter of the week is the right direction for you to go. From here on out, for you ABCs mean *A Better Course*.

APPENDIX A

Kindergarten Read-Alouds for Print Referencing

When choosing read-alouds that offer engaging opportunities for referencing print, books with "high print salience"—a considerable number of interesting print features—offer the most support. Often, text is embedded in illustrations in the form of speech bubbles, thought balloons, labels, or signs. Text that appears as separate from illustrations might change font, size, or color to reflect sound or emotion (Zucker, Ward, and Justice 2009). Of course, almost any well-loved read-aloud could be used for print referencing, but these are some of our favorites.

Title	Author/Illustrator	Publisher
All the World	Liz Garton Scanlon/ Marla Frazee	Beach Lane Books
Along a Long Road	Frank Viva	Little, Brown and Company
Aunt Harriet's Underground Railroad in the Sky	Faith Ringgold	Dragonfly Books
The Baby BeeBee Bird	Diane Redfield Massie/ Steven Kellogg	HarperCollins
Bad Bye, Good Bye	Deborah Underwood	Houghton Mifflin Harcourt
Bark George	Jules Feiffer	Scholastic
Bigmama's	Donald Crews	Greenwillow Books
Brown Bear, Brown Bear, What Do You See?	Bill Martin Jr./ Eric Carle	HarperCollins

(continues)

Title	Author/Illustrator	Publisher
The Bunnies Are Not in Their Beds	Marisabina Russo	Random House Children's Books
The Carrot Seed	Ruth Krauss	HarperCollins
Cat Says Meow	Michael Arndt	Chronicle
Color Zoo	Lois Ehler	HarperCollins
Each Peach Pear Plum	Janet and Allan Ahlberg	Puffin
Everyone Can Learn to Ride a Bicycle	Chris Raschka	Schwartz & Wade Books
From Head to Toe	Eric Carle	HarperCollins
Good Night, Gorilla	Peggy Rathmann	Puffin
In the Tall, Tall Grass	Denise Fleming	Henry Holt and Company
Joseph Had a Little Overcoat	Simms Taback	Viking
Kitten's First Full Moon	Kevin Henkes	HarperCollins
Mice and Beans	Pam Munoz Ryan/ Joe Cepeda	Scholastic
The Napping House	Audrey Wood/ Don Wood	HMH Books for Young Readers
The Neighborhood Mother Goose	Nina Crews	Greenwillow Books
Noisy Nora	Rosemary Wells	Puffin Books
Oh, No!	Candace Fleming/ Eric Rohrmann	Schwartz & Wade Books
One	Kathryn Otoshi	KO Kids Books
Owl Babies	Martin Waddell	Candlewick Press
Pete's a Pizza	William Steig	HarperCollins

Title	Author/Illustrator	Publisher
School Bus	Donald Crews	HarperCollins
Shortcut	Donald Crews	Greenwillow Books
Silly Chicken	Rukhsana Khan/ Yummee Kong	Viking Juvenile
Slow Loris	Alexis Deacon	Kane/Miller Book Publishers
The Snowy Day	Ezra Jack Keats	Viking
We're Going on a Bear Hunt	Michael Rosen/Helen Oxenbury	Aladdin Paperbacks
What Pete Ate from A–Z (Really!)	Maira Kalman	Puffin Books
Yo? Yes!	Chris Raschka	Scholastic
Zero	Kathryn Otoshi	KO Kids Books
Zoo Looking	Mem Fox/ Candace Whitman	Mondo
The Elephant and Piggie Book Series	Mo Willems	Hyperion Books for Children
The Pigeon Book Series	Mo Willems	Hyperion Books for Children

APPENDIX B

Kindergarten Read-Alouds That Support Wordplay and Poetry

Title	Author/ Illustrator	Publisher
17 Kings and 42 Elephants	Margaret Mahy/ Patricia MacCarthy	Dial
The Adventures of Isabel	Ogden Nash/Bridget Starr Taylor	Sourcebooks Jabberwocky
Arroz con Leche: Popular Songs and Rhymes from Latin America	Lulu Delacre	Scholastic
Charlie Parker Played Be Bop	Chris Raschka	Scholastic
Chicken Soup with Rice	Maurice Sendak	HarperCollins
The Circus Ship	Chris VanDusen	Candlewick
Eating the Alphabet: Fruits and Vegetables from A to Z	Lois Ehlert	Harcourt
Flower Garden	Eve Bunting/ Kathryn Hewitt	HMH Books for Young Readers
Fox in Socks	Dr. Seuss	Random House
He's Got the Whole World in His Hands	Kadir Nelson	Dial
A House Is a House for Me	Mary Ann Hoberman	Viking Press
I Live in Music	Ntozake Shange/ Romare Beardon	Steward, Tabori & Chang
In the Tall, Tall Grass	Denise Fleming	Holt
It Begins with an A	Stephanie Calmenson/ Marisabina Russo	Hyperion

(continues)

Title	Author/ Illustrator	Publisher
Keisha Ann Can!	Daniel Kirk	Putnam Juvenile
Laughing Tomatoes and Other Spring Poems	Francisco Alarcon/ Maya Christina Gonzalez	Children's Book Press
Lineup for Yesterday	Ogden Nash/ C. F. Payne	Creative Editions
Little Book of Alliterations	Felix Archer	21st Century
Mean Jean the Recess Queen	Alexis O'Neill/ Laura Huliska-Beith	Scholastic
Meet Danitra Brown	Nikki Grimes/ Floyd Cooper	HarperCollins
Mike and the Bike	Michael Ward/ Bob Thompson	Monkey Feathers Books
Mike and the Bike Meet Lucille and the Wheel	Michael Ward/ Bob Thompson	Monkey Feathers Books
Moira's Birthday	Robert Munsch	Annick Press
One Sun: A Book of Terse Verse	Bruce McMillan	Holiday House
One Was Johnny: A Counting Book	Maurice Sendak	HarperCollins
Pierre: A Cautionary Tale	Maurice Sendak	HarperCollins
¡Pío Peep! Traditional Rhymes in Spanish	Alma Flor Ada/ Vivi Escriva	HarperFestival
A Pocketful of Poems	Nikki Grimes	Clarion Books
Polkabats and Octopus Slacks	Calef Brown	HMH Books for Young Readers
Rap a Tap Tap: Here's Bojangles — Think of That!	Leo and Diane Dillon	Blue Sky Press
Room on the Broom	Julia Donaldson/ Axel Scheffler	Puffin

Title	Author/ Illustrator	Publisher
The Tale of Custard the Dragon	Ogden Nash/ Lynn Munsinger	Little, Brown
There Was An Old Lady Who Swallowed a Fly	Simms Taback	Viking
Three Little Kittens	Paul Galdone	HMH Books for Young Readers
Uno Dos Tres: One Two Three	Pat Mora/ Barbara Lavalee	HMH Books for Young Readers
What Do You Do with a Kangaroo?	Mercer Mayer	Scholastic
When Gorilla Goes Walking	Nikki Grimes/ Shane Evans	Orchard Books
Zin! Zin! Zin! A Violin	Lloyd Moss/ Marjorie Priceman	Aladdin
Llama Llama... Book Series	Anna Dewdney	Viking

REFERENCES

Adams, M. 1990. *Beginning to Read: Thinking and Learning about Print.* Cambridge, MA: MIT Press.

———. 2010. "The Relation Between Alphabetic Basics, Word Recognition, and Reading." In *What Research Has to Say About Reading Instruction,* 4th ed., edited by S. Samuels and A. Farstrup. Newark, DE: International Reading Association.

Blaiklock, K. E. 2004. "The Importance of Letter Knowledge in the Relationship between Phonological Awareness and Reading." *Journal of Research in Reading* 27: 36–57.

Bowles, R. P., J. M. Pentimonti, H. K. Gerde, and J. J. Montroy. 2014. "Item Response Analysis of Uppercase and Lowercase Letter Name Knowledge." *Journal of Psychoeducational Assessment* 32 (2): 146–56.

Bredekamp, S., ed. 1987. *Developmentally Appropriate Practice in Early Childhood Programs Serving Children from Birth Through Age 8.* Washington, DC: NAEYC.

Brookfield, J., N. Norris, M. Baldo, M. Brown, and L. K. Brummell. 2013. *Embedding Effective Instruction in Games to Teach Code-Related Early Literacy Skills.* Paper presented at 58th Annual Conference of the International Reading Association, San Antonio.

Burgess, S., and C. Lonigan. 1998. "Bidirectional Relations of Phonological Sensitivity and Pre-Reading Abilities: Evidence from a Preschool Sample." *Journal of Experimental Child Psychology* 70: 117–41.

Bus, A. G., and M. van IJzendoorn. 1999. "Phonological Awareness and Early Reading: A Meta-analysis of Experimental Training Studies." *Journal of Educational Psychology* 91: 403–14.

Carnine, D. W., J. Silbert, E. J. Kame'enui, and S. G. Tarver. 2009. *Direct Instruction Reading,* 5th ed. New York: Pearson.

Catts, H. W., M. E. Fey, J. B. Tomblin, and X. Zhang. 2002. "A Longitudinal Investigation of Reading Outcomes in Children with Language Impairment." *Journal of Speech, Language, and Hearing Research* 45: 1142–57.

Clarke, L. K. 1988. "Invented Versus Traditional Spelling in First Graders' Writings: Effects on Learning to Spell and Read." *Research in the Teaching of English* 22: 281–309.

Copple, C., and S. Bredekamp, eds. 2010. *Developmentally Appropriate Practice in Early Childhood Programs Serving Children from Birth Through Age 8*, 3d ed. Washington, DC: NAEYC.

Craig, S. A. 2006. "The Effects of an Adapted Interactive Writing Intervention on Kindergarten Children's Phonological Awareness, Spelling, and Early Reading Development: A Contextualized Approach to Instruction." *Journal of Educational Psychology* 98 (4): 714–31.

de Abreu, M., and C. Cardoso-Martins. 1998. "Alphabetic Access Route in Beginning Reading Acquisition in Portuguese: The Role of Letter-Name Knowledge." *Reading & Writing* 10: 85–104.

Ehri, L. 1983. "A Critique of Five Studies Related to Letter-Name Knowledge and Learning to Read." In *Reading Research Revisited*, edited by L. M. Gentile, M. L. Kamil, and J. S. Blanchard, 143–53. Columbus, OH: Merrill.

Ehri, L., and S. McCormick. 2013. "Phases of Word Learning: Implications for Instruction with Delayed and Disabled Readers." In *Theoretical Models and Processes of Reading*, 6th ed., edited by D. Alvermann, N. Unrau, and R. Ruddell, 339–61. Newark, DE: International Reading Association.

Ehri, L., S. Nunes, S. Stahl, and D. Willows. 2001. "Systematic Phonics Instruction Helps Students Learn to Read: Evidence from the National Reading Panel's Meta-Analysis." *Review of Educational Research* 71: 393–447.

Ehri, L. C., and T. Roberts. 2006. "The Roots of Learning to Read and Write: Acquisition of Letters and Phonemic Awareness." In *Handbook of Early Literacy Research*, Vol. 2, edited by D. K. Dickinson and S. B. Neuman, 113–31. New York: Guilford.

Evans, M., M. Bell, D. Shaw, S. Moretti, and S. Page. 2006. "Letter Names, Letter Sounds, and Phonological Awareness: An Examination of Kindergarten Children across Letters and of Letters across Children." *Reading and Writing* 19: 959–89.

Foy, J. G., and V. Mann. 2006. "Changes in Letter Sound Knowledge Are Associated with Development of Phonological Awareness in Pre-school Children." *Journal of Research in Reading* 29 (2): 143–61.

Gibson, E. J., and H. Levin. 1975. *The Psychology of Reading*. Cambridge, MA: MIT Press.

Hammill, D. D. 2004. "What We Know about Correlates of Reading." *Exceptional Children* 70: 453–68.

Hayes, D. 1982. "Handwriting Practice: The Effects of Perceptual Prompts." *Journal of Educational Research* 75: 169–72.

Huang, F., and M. Invernizzi. 2012. "The Association of Age and Early Literacy Outcomes." *Journal of Educational Research* 105: 431–41.

Institute of Education Sciences. 2006. What Works Clearinghouse. "Phonological Awareness Training Plus Letter Knowledge Training." Available at http://ies.ed.gov/ncee/wwc/interventionreport.aspx?sid=376.

———. 2007. What Works Clearinghouse. "Direct Instruction." Available at: http://ies.ed.gov/ncee/WWC/interventionreport.aspx?sid=139.

Jones, C., and D. R. Reutzel. 2012. "Enhanced Alphabet Knowledge Instruction: Exploring a Change of Frequency, Focus, and Distributed Cycles of Review." *Reading Psychology* 33 (5).

Jones, C. D., S. K. Clark, and D. R. Reutzel. 2012. "Enhancing Alphabet Knowledge Instruction: Research Implications and Practical Strategies for Early Childhood Educators." Teal Faculty Publications, Paper 404. Logan, UT: Utah State University. Available at http://digitalcommons.usu.edu /teal_facpub/404.

Juel, C. 1988. "Learning to Read and Write: A Longitudinal Study of 54 Children from First Through Fourth Grades." *Journal of Educational Psychology* 80 (4): 437–47.

Juel, C., P. Griffin, and P. Gough. 1986. "Acquisition of Literacy: A Longitudinal Study of Children in First and Second Grades." *Journal of Educational Psychology* 78 (4): 243–55.

Justice, L. M., A. S. McGinty, S. B. Piasta, J. N. Kaderavek, and X. Fan. 2010. "Print-Focused Read-Alouds in Preschool Classrooms: Intervention Effectiveness and Moderators of Child Outcomes." *Language, Speech, and Hearing Services in Schools* 41: 504–20.

Justice, L. M., K. Pence, R. Bowles, and A. Wiggins, A. 2006. "An Investigation of Four Hypotheses Concerning the Order by Which 4-Year-Old Children Learn the Alphabet Letters." *Early Childhood Research Quarterly* 21: 374–89.

Lafferty, A. E., S. Gray, and M. J. Wilcox. 2005. "Teaching Alphabet Knowledge to Pre-School Children with Developmental Language Delay and with Typical Language Development." *Child Language Teaching and Therapy* 21: 263–77.

Lomax, R. G., and L. M. McGee. 1987. "Young Children's Concepts about Print and Reading: Toward a Model of Reading Acquisition." *Reading Research Quarterly* 22: 237–56.

Lonigan, C. J., S. R. Burgess, and J. L. Anthony. 2000. "Development of Emergent Literacy and Early Reading Skills in Preschool Children: Evidence from a Latent-Variable Longitudinal Study." *Developmental Psychology* 36: 596–613.

Martinelli, M., and K. Mraz. 2012. *Smarter Charts K–2: Optimizing an Instructional Staple to Create Independent Readers and Writers.* Portsmouth, NH: Heinemann.

Mason, J. 1980. "When Do Children Begin to Learn to Read: An Exploration of Four-Year-Old Children's Letter and Word Reading Competencies." *Reading Research Quarterly* 15: 203–27.

McBride-Chang, C. 1999. "The ABCs of the ABCs: The Development of Letter-Name and Letter-Sound Knowledge." *Merrill-Palmer Quarterly* 45: 285–308.

McGee, L., and D. Richgels. 2012. *Literacy's Beginnings: Supporting Young Readers and Writers*, 6th ed. New York: Pearson.

Melby-Lervåg, M., S.-A. H. Lyster, and C. Hulme. 2012. "Phonological Skills and Their Role in Learning to Read: A Meta-Analytic Review." *Psychological Bulletin* 138 (2): 322–52.

National Assessment of Educational Progress. 2013. "The Nation's Report Card." Available at http://www.nationsreportcard.gov/reading_math_2013.

National Early Literacy Panel. 2008. *Developing Early Literacy: Report of the National Early Literacy Panel.* Washington, DC: National Institute for Literacy.

National Governors Association Center for Best Practices (NGA Center) and Council of Chief State School Officers (CCSSO). 2011. *Common Core State Standards for English Language Arts and Literacy.* Washington, DC: NGA Center and CCSSO.

National Reading Panel. 2000. *Teaching Children to Read: An Evidence-Based Assessment of the Scientific Research Literature on Reading and Its Implications for Reading Instruction.* (NIH Publication No. 00-4769.) Washington, DC: U.S. Government Printing Office.

Phillips, B. M., and S. B. Piasta. 2013. "Phonological Awareness and Alphabet Knowledge: Key Precursors and Instructional Targets to Promote Reading Success." In *Early Childhood Literacy: The National Early Literacy Panel and Beyond*, edited by T. Shanahan and C. J. Lonigan, 95–116. Baltimore: Paul H. Brookes.

Piasta, S., and R. K. Wagner. 2010. "Learning Letter Names and Sounds: Effects of Instruction, Letter Type, and Phonological Processing Skill." *Journal of Experimental Child Psychology* 105: 324–44.

Piasta, S. B., Y. Petscher, and L. M. Justice. 2012. "How Many Letter Sounds Should Preschoolers in Public Programs Know? The Diagnostic Efficiency of Various Preschool Letter-Naming Benchmarks for Predicting First-Grade Literacy Achievement." *Journal of Educational Psychology* 104 (4): 945–58.

Read, C. 1971. "Pre-School Children's Knowledge of English Phonology." *Harvard Educational Review* 41: 1–34.

Richgels, D. J. 1986. "Beginning First Graders' 'Invented Spelling' Ability and Their Performance in Functional Classroom Writing Activities." *Early Childhood Research Quarterly* 1 (1): 85–97.

———. 1995. "Invented Spelling Ability and Printed Word Learning in Kindergarten." *Reading Research Quarterly* 30: 96–109.

———. 2001. "Invented Spelling, Phonemic Awareness, and Writing Instruction." In *Handbook of Early Literacy Research*, edited by S. B. Newman and D. Dickinson, 142–55. New York: Guilford.

Roberts, T. 2009. *No Limits to Literacy for Preschool English Learners*. Thousand Oaks, CA: Corwin.

———. 2013. "The Roots of Learning to Read and Write: Acquisition of Letters and Phonemic Awareness in English Language Learner and English Only Children." Paper presented at the 57th Annual Conference of the International Reading Association, May 2013, San Antonio, TX.

Roberts, T., and P. Vadasy. 2013. *Cognitive Processes Involved in Alphabet Learning: Implications for Instruction*. Paper presented at the 63rd Annual Conference of the Literacy Research Association, December 2013, Dallas, TX.

Scanlon, D. M., K. L. Anderson, and J. M. Sweeney. 2010. *Early Intervention for Reading Difficulties: The Interactive Strategies Approach*. New York: Guilford.

Scarborough, H. 1998. "Early Identification of Children at Risk for Reading Disabilities." In *Specific Reading Disability*, edited by B. Shapiro, P. Accardo, and A. Capute, 75–119. Timonium, MD: York Press.

Schatschneider, C., K. Fletcher, D. Francis, C. Carlson, and B. Foorman. 2004. "Kindergarten Prediction of Reading Skills: A Longitudinal Comparative Analysis." *Journal of Educational Psychology* 96: 265–82.

Schickedanz, J. A., and R. M. Casbergue. 2009. *Writing in Preschool: Learning to Orchestrate Meaning and Marks*, 2d ed. Newark, DE: International Reading Association.

Share, D. L. 2004. "Knowing Letter Names and Learning Letter Sounds: A Causal Connection." *Journal of Experimental Child Psychology* 88: 213–33.

Share, D. L., A. F. Jorm, R. Maclean, and R. Matthews. 1987. "Sources of Individual Differences in Reading Acquisition." *Journal of Educational Psychology* 76 (6): 1309–24.

Smythe, P. C., R. G. Stennett, M. Hardy, and H. R. Wilson. 1971. "Developmental Patterns in Elemental Skills: Knowledge of Uppercase and Lowercase Letter Names." *Journal of Reading Behavior* 3: 24–33.

Stahl, S. A., and B. A. Murray. 1994. "Defining Phonological Awareness and Its Relationship to Early Reading." *Journal of Educational Psychology* 86 (2): 221–34.

Teale, W. H. 1995. "Young Children and Reading: Trends Across the 20th Century." *Journal of Education* 177: 95–126.

Teale, W. H., J. L. Hoffman, K. A. Paciga, J. Garrette, S. Richardson, and C. Berkel. 2009. "Early Literacy: Then and Now." In *Changing Literacies for Changing Times*, edited by Y. Goodman and J. Hoffman, 76–97. New York: Routledge.

Teale, W. H., K. A. Paciga, and J. L. Hoffman. 2010. "What It Takes in Early Schooling to Have Adolescents Who Are Skilled and Eager Readers and Writers." In *Interdisciplinary Perspectives on Learning to Read: Culture, Cognition, and Pedagogy*, edited by K. Hall, U. Goswami, C. Harrison, S. Ellis, and J. Soler, 151–63. London: Routledge.

Treiman, R., R. Tincoff, K. Rodriguez, A. Mouzaki, and D. Francis. 1998. "The Foundations of Literacy: Learning the Sounds of Letters." *Child Development* 69: 1524–40.

Turnbull, K. L. P., R. P. Bowles, L. E. Skibbe, L. M. Justice, and A. K. Wiggins. 2010. "Theoretical Explanations for Preschoolers' Lowercase Alphabet Knowledge." *Journal of Speech, Language, and Hearing Research* 53: 1757–68.

University of Illinois at Chicago. 2008. "UIC Early Reading First." Available at http://www.uic.edu/educ/erf/.

U.S. Department of Education. 2014. Programs. "Early Reading First." Available at http://www2.ed.gov/programs/earlyreading/index.html.

U.S. Department of Health and Human Services. 2014. Head Start. "T/TA Resources." Available at http://eclkc.ohs.acf.hhs.gov/hslc/tta-system /teaching/eecd/domains%20of%20child%20development/literacy/edudev _art_00012_061405.html#Abc.

Vellutino, F. R., and D. M. Scanlon. 1987. "Phonological Coding, Phonological Awareness, and Reading Ability: Evidence from a Longitudinal and Experimental Study." *Merrill-Palmer Quarterly* 33: 321–63.

Vukelich, C., and J. Christie. 2009. *Building a Foundation for Preschool Literacy*, 2d ed. Newark, DE: International Reading Association.

Wagner, R. K., J. K. Torgesen, and C. A. Rashotte. 1994. "Development of Reading Related Phonological Processing Abilities: New Evidence of Bidirectional Causality from a Latent Variable Longitudinal Study." *Journal of Educational Psychology* 69: 36–39.

Walsh, D., G. Price, and M. Gillingham. 1988. "The Critical but Transitory Importance of Letter Naming." *Reading Research Quarterly* 23: 108–22.

Whitehurst, G., and C. Lonigan. 1998. "Child Development and Emergent Literacy." *Child Development* 69 (3): 848–72.

Worden, P. E., and W. Boettcher. 1990. "Young Children's Acquisition of Alphabet Knowledge." *Journal of Reading Behavior* 22: 277–95.

Zucker, T., A. Ward, and L. Justice. 2009. "Print Referencing during Read-Alouds: A Technique for Increasing Emergent Readers' Print Knowledge. *Reading Teacher* 63 (1): 62–72.